PORTSMOUTH
THE WAY IT WAS

Island History
Volume III

Ellen Fulcher Cloud

HERITAGE BOOKS
2011

HERITAGE BOOKS

AN IMPRINT OF HERITAGE BOOKS, INC.

Books, CDs, and more—Worldwide

For our listing of thousands of titles see our website
at
www.HeritageBooks.com

Published 2011 by
HERITAGE BOOKS, INC.
Publishing Division
100 Railroad Ave. #104
Westminster, Maryland 21157

Copyright © 1996 Ellen Fulcher Cloud

International Standard Book Numbers
Paperbound: 978-0-7884-3830-1
Clothbound: 978-0-7884-8937-2

PORTSMOUTH
THE WAY IT WAS

by

Ellen Fulcher Cloud

ISLAND HISTORY

IN MEMORY OF
MRS. MATTIE DALY GILGO
8 NOV. 1885 - 20 FEB. 1976

Whose interview inspired this book.

*photo from
Julian Gilgo Collection*

TABLE OF CONTENTS

PREFACE

Portsmouth Island is a place that holds many childhood memories for me. I remember our many family outings, when daddy would load us all on the "Aleta" and slowly make our way across Ocracoke Inlet to the Coast Guard Station on Portsmouth. We usually had sandwiches, fried chicken and potato salad, as well as iced down drinks and buckets for picking dewberries. We would dock near the station and have our lunch on the porch of the station before walking on to the village where mama and daddy would visit with the residents. We kids were hurrying off into the bushes and marshes to pick dewberries. There, were the biggest berries ever to ripen on a vine. We usually ate as many as we put in the buckets and it was nothing to pick a 10 qt. water bucket full apiece. Needless to say we went home sick every time.

In those days I guess, the greatest thing about Portsmouth was the size of the berries. I don't ever remember being bit by flies or mosquitoes, though we probably were. As years went by and Ocracoke started growing and attracting more and more tourists, the greatest thing about Portsmouth was, there were no tourists, it was so quiet it seemed to deafen you. People still sat on their porches and visited with each other. There seemed to be no time for that at Ocracoke any-more. I loved to wander down the narrow paths and listen to the birds and an occasional snap of a twig as a rabbit ran into the bushes.

I left Ocracoke in 1963 and returned in 1984. I visited Portsmouth only two times in those 21 years, but bought every book printed about it and saved every newspaper or maga-zine article.

Since returning to Ocracoke I have visited Portsmouth as often as possible. The last residents have left and the island is in fact a "ghost town." Many of the old homes on the island have collapsed or are in a serious state of decay. In the past the houses could be leased for as little as ten dollars a year. Sometimes as many as two years passed before a lessee visited the island, and little or no money was spent to maintain the structures. Since the leases were let on a yearly basis, lessees were hesitant to invest much in the buildings for fear their lease would not be renewed the next year.

Because of the loss of such buildings, the Cape Lookout National Park cancelled all yearly leases and started a new program. Many old lessees who did maintain their property were former Portsmouth residents and the loss of their leases was devastating. The houses are let now for a twenty year term. The lessee must restore the structure as well as any out buildings and fences, to an original state and then maintain them. All time, money and materials are credited to an annual rental fee.

Often more than 100 applicants are received for perhaps four to five houses. Since applicants must have some

Friends and former residents of Portsmouth relax on the porch of our leased house.

experience and knowledge of historical restoration and be willing to put time and money into the project. Few completed applications are received and from these, perhaps one or two contracts are signed.

I was fortunate to have friends that were willing to join me in a venture to secure such a lease. Restoration is well on its way and we get to spend a lot of time there. Often friends, who are former residents of Portsmouth join us on our visits to the Island. What a pleasure it is to sit on the porch and listen to them reminisce about their years spent there.

The program seems to be the best way to maintain the buildings. Many structures being offered are not being leased because of their severe deteriorated state. Others such as the church, Coast Guard Station and ranger quarters are not offered for lease. The C.G. station is used for storage of park equipment. The ranger station and church are in serious need of a friend. The park either for lack of money and, or lack of interest has neglected them for many years.

There is a part time employee of the park who works three days a week mowing grass and clearing brush. He is a qualified restoration specialist, but such work is not included in his work title.

There is a volunteer program in which the park allows volunteers to actually live on the island for one to three months during the tourist season and act as caretakers and guides for the park. This program has been very successful since there are scores of people who visit the island during the season.

Automobiles are not allowed in the village which certainly is a plus for a walk. No phones, no electricity, and no gift shops are part of the charm.

Yes, Portsmouth is a wonderful place and the more time I spend there the more I hate to leave. There is so much history connected with this place that I am almost always in a state of awe. Every ruin I find, every grave I locate, and every piece of pottery I find on the water's edge inspires another research project. I have to know to whom it belonged, who was there before them, what kind of life they lived and why they were there.

Recently members of the "Friends Of Portsmouth Island" supervised by Dave Frum, who is employed by the park, cleared the old "Straight Road." This is the same horse and cart road made in the 1700's that runs the whole length of the island. The road starts at Haulover Point and runs down past the "Middle Settlement" and on to "Sheep Island", located near the south end of the island. Both of these communities were settled in the mid 1700's. There are no old homes left in either place but the ruins are reminders of days gone by.

An old cemetery located between The Middle Settle ment and Sheep Island has long since been washed away along with the earth on which it was located. Just recently a group of us, with the use of gigs, located some of the tombs buried on the bottom of Warren Gilgo's Creek. We placed the tombs on the shore where we will clean and restore them. Many were broken and we hope to find the other pieces as well as the rest of the tombs. One undamaged tomb was that of William Austin who died in 1832 at the age of forty one.

Many people believe that the ghost of former residents still remain on the island. One believer stated that he had heard and seen things on Portsmouth that he has told no one for fear they would think he was crazy. He insists that "Portsmouth is not dead, Portsmouth lives on."

Today, the tourists have found Portsmouth. There are few times from early spring to late fall that you won't see at least half dozen people when visiting the island, but they don't stay long. The mosquitoes and flies run them away. I enjoy

Portsmouth most in the late fall and winter months, when there are neither bugs or tourists, but I have to admit that it's great in the summer also.

After knowing and enjoying Portsmouth as a child, I thank God every day that it is a part of the Cape Lookout National Park and therefore protected from development. If it were not for the Park Service, both Ocracoke and Portsmouth would probably be as congested as Nags Head and Atlantic Beach.

There has been much written about Portsmouth Island, but very little about its rich history or everyday life as it took place. This book begins with a little history of the early years at Portsmouth and the activities and commerce carried on there in the late 1700's and early 1800's.

Part II of this book jumps right into real life on Portsmouth in the late 1800's and early 1900's as recalled by Mrs. Mattie Daly Gilgo, a former resident of Portsmouth Island.

ACKNOWLEDGEMENTS

First I want to thank Julian Gilgo for letting me borrow the tapes of his interview with his grandmother, Mrs. Mattie Daly Gilgo. I thank Hazel Arthur, Leona Gilgo, Martha Day and Cape Lookout National Seashore for letting me copy their photos and Paulette Chitwood for copying them. Cecil Gilgo for taking the time to talk with me about his time spent on the Island and to help me locate the different home sites. Thanks to Bill Dudley for sharing his information on Augustus Dudley and a special thanks to Agnes Wren for her continuing support.

EFC

CHAPTER 1

THE ISLAND

Portsmouth is an island on the Outer Banks of North Carolina in Carteret County, and part of the Cape Lookout National Park. It is located 6 miles southwest from the village of Ocracoke and separated from Ocracoke Island by Ocracoke Inlet. It was named for Portsmouth, England and established in 1753 by North Carolina legislative act.

In the late 1700's and early 1800's Portsmouth was a thriving sea port and the center of shipping and trade with the outside world. Ocracoke Inlet was the only outlet for ships from the ports on the Neuse, Roanoke and Pamlico Rivers. However passage through the inlet with a loaded vessel was impossible because of shallow water and treacherous shoals. For this reason it was necessary for great ships anchored in the roads of Ocracoke Inlet to transfer part or all of their cargo to another vessel in order to lighten the ship, thus allowing it to cross the bar. This act was known as lightering.

Ships sometimes had to ride at anchor for days waiting for vessels to lighter them, which left them at the mercy of pirates and more often severe weather.

The General Assembly of North Carolina on March 27,1753, passed legislation entitled "An act for appointing and laying out a town on Core Banks, near Ocacock Inlet, in Carteret County." The act was to encourage the development of a harbor with warehouses and encourage lightering businesses. The town was to be named Portsmouth. Fifty acres were laid off and divided into half acre lots. For twenty shillings any person could purchase a lot if he was willing to be an inhabitant of the island and build a house or warehouse of at least twenty by sixteen feet. Within five years Portsmouth had been laid out as planned and was inhabited.

Portsmouth Island itself did not become the center of shipping as expected. The core of activity was actually on an island in Pamlico Sound two miles North of the village of Portsmouth and 4.9 miles west of the village of Ocracoke, once called Old Rock. The name was changed to Shell Castle Rock in 1789 by the owners John Gray Blount and John Wallace when they established several commercial businesses there.

John Gray Blount was a successful businessman in the merchandising business and had the largest shipping company in the State. He and John Wallace were partners in the enterprises established on Shell Castle. Blount was the financial backer and Wallace was proprietor of the operation, which consisted of warehouses, wharfs, a tavern, store, fish factory, lightering business, a grist mill, windmill and three dwellings.

By 1806 commerce had grown so that a custom house was established and called District of Ocracoke, with James Taylor appointed the first collector. It got it's name from Ocracoke Inlet, for it was never located at Ocracoke, nor did any of the collectors reside at Ocracoke, but rather on Portsmouth or Shell Castle. The district was given the use of a revenue cutter "Governor Williams*."

As early as 1736 Governor George Burrengton saw the importance of Ocracoke Inlet when he wrote;

"Ocracoke inlet has two channels which do not shift or change--inside the South End of the Island lyes the Harbor which has convenient places to careen ships, wood and good fresh water in abundance. A small Fort mounted with some cannons would prove in time of war, a sufficient Security to the shipping in

* Correspondance of Secretary of Treasurey with Collector of Port, 1789-1833 National Archives of History, Washington , DC.

the harbor and house on land. I observe a certain spot of land from whence a Bullet shot out of a great gun would reach the bar. Ocracoke Island is an airy and healthy place abounding with excellent fish and wild foul. If a collector is settled at Ocracoke it will be difficult to bring into that part of the province any prohibited goods, without paying the King's Duty, because all vessels that come down from the rivers or sail from sea are to be seen a long time before they enter harbor."

20 July 1736   George Burrengton

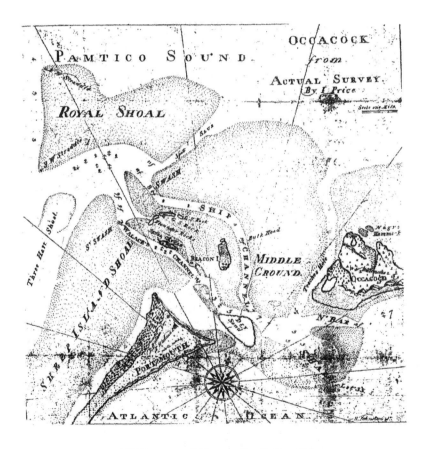

1795 map of Ocracoke Inlet, Price

CHAPTER 2

MARINE HOSPITAL

Shipping became so great through Ocracoke Inlet that by 1820, a marine hospital was established on Portsmouth. The first Hospital was but a shack, as described in a letter to the Collector of Port dated 1831. (See copy pg. 9) In 1845 a new hospital, very modern for it's time, was built by the government, near the site of the old one. The structure was two-storied, with ten rooms downstairs and two upstairs. There were seven fireplaces, two porches and a dock for unloading supplies and patients.

The Hospital was discontinued before the Civil War and was used as housing for a company of Confederate Soldiers from Greenville, NC, known as the "Tar River Boy's", who were stationed at Portsmouth in 1861.

After the forts were taken at Hatteras, Portsmouth was evacuated, and the Union Troops soon took command of the hospital and put Captain James W. Davis in charge. The hospital was used to treat the sick and wounded Union troops in the area.

The Army Signal Corps occupied the building in 1876. William Daly, father of Mrs. Mattie Gilgo, (interview in this book) was one of the first employees at the Post. This operation was discontinued in 1883 and the building was once again vacant. The building was burned sometime in the late 1890's.

The following letter was sent to the Collector of the Port of Ocracoke, appointing Dr. John W. Potts physician of the marine hospital.

Treasury Department
Feb. 11, 1828

Sir;

Upon an inspection of the proposals for establishing a Marine Hospital in your district, which accompanied your letter of the 30th, it appears that the one made by Dr. John W. Potts is considerably the lowest, and as he has been strongly recommended by Messrs Bryan and Hall of the House of Representatives, you may consider yourself as authorized to enter into a formal contract in writing with Doctor Potts for the term of two years for the sum of fifteen hundred dollars per annum, to be paid Quarterly by your draft on the collector of New Bern. Care must be taken to select the most healthy and convenient situation for the hospital and that the contract expressly stipulate that all sick and disabled seamen applying for the benefit of the hospital, shall be provided with board, lodging, nursing, medical aid and medicines, and that the food shall be of good quality. You will be pleased to in-form Dr. Potts that his proposal has been accepted, and that agreeable to usage in such cases, he will be required to give bond and Security for faithful performance of contract. A certified copy of which, when executed, must be transmitted to this office.

I am respectfully
your obedt. Servant
Richard Rush

CHAPTER 3

DR. SAMUEL DUDLEY

Dr. Samuel Dudley was the second physician in charge of the new hospital, taking over a contract issued to Dr. John W. Potts, who served as physician for just a short while. Dr. Dudley was soon to become one of the island's wealthiest residents. The creek on which he built his home was called Doctor's Creek.

The Enrollments of Vessels at Port Ocracoke list Dudley as owner of seven ships between the years 1833 and 1839. He also owned a large tract of land. He deeded part to the trustees of the Methodist Church, for construction of a church.

Members of the board of trustees formed in July of 1840 were Dr.Dudley, Wallace Whitehurst, William C. Dixon, Wallis Styron and Thomas W. Styron.

Most records show Dr. Dudley as being an upstanding citizen who was respected and looked up to by the citizens of Portsmouth and Ocracoke. On many occasions, Dr. Dudley traveled to Ocracoke to provide medical care for residents of the Island, and at times residents of Ocracoke went to Portsmouth for his care.

Nevertheless Dr. Dudley was not respected by all. Records show that his medical knowledge as well as his feelings for humanity were questioned at times. Reference here is made to a letter from one, Joseph B. Hurtow to Collector of Customs dated 24th Feb. 1831.

In addition, in 1836 Thomas Robinson, then Collector of Customs, was brought to court by Dudley with charges of slander made in a newspaper published in Washington, NC. The charges were not taken seriously, for Dr. Dudley remained the Physician* on Portsmouth Island, until his death. He was buried on Portsmouth, but around 1920 his heirs came and removed his remains to the mainland.

I have included here on the next few pages, just for the record, copies of the documents questioning Dr. Dudley's integrity, followed by abstracts of Documentation Papers of vessels he owned.

*   Dudley's house was located on the East side of Doctor's Creek. It is described by Mrs. Gilgo in part II of this book as being like two houses together with a large chimney between them. Court records (pg 15) states there was a hospital connecting the doctor's residence in 1836. It appears that the conditions at the hospital in 1831 (described on page 11) were so bad that Dr. Dudley may have opened part of his home or added to his home in order to provide better service to his patients until the new hospital was constructed in 1845. Remnants of old medicine bottles with Dudley in raised letter can be seen at the edge of Doctor's Creek.

LETTER TO COLLECTOR OF CUSTOMS
OCRACOKE DISTRICT
24th Feb. 1831

Three or four years ago the first contract was made for a Marine Infirmary near Ocracoke, N.C. and my half-brother, James W. Potts was the contractor at $1500 per anl. There were two other bids one of $2,000 and the other of $2,500. Dr. Potts soon found that the trouble and expense greatly exceeded his expectations and after a eighteen months, became very devious of surrendering the contract.

About that time Dudley visited Ocracoke, in quest of a school of small children and offered to take the remainder of the contract off Dr. Potts hands, he readily gave it up to him, and perhaps a hundred dollars worth of medicine into the bargain, and now Dudley becomes known as Dr. Dudley--and that the hospital was discontinued except as far as this--that Dudley was to render, a bill for every particular case, to be charged as the Department had regulated. If seamen knew that the hospital contract had been renewed with Dudley until June next, they must have been unwilling to take their chances of treatment with him, for in the port of Washington, there was the last year and perhaps the year before, considerable sickness among seamen. Their condition when sick in our little town, is truly distressing. If they live in the filthy brothers into which they are generally placed, neglect and suffering is their certain doom: if they die, they die alone, or among the outcasts from Heaven and earth.

As to the hospital at (Port) Ocracoke, a small wooden house has been rented and occupied for the purpose at $30 to $40 per year. The house stands about two feet above the level of the ocean and not to far from it's margin, upon the Portsmouth Banks and on the naked sands, without the benefit of shade. The house itself is 16 to 18 feet by 20 or 22 feet in size, without plastering or as I believe glass windows. About six cots, a pine table or two and a few benches or chairs, and the furniture of the hospital has been described. There being no cistern to contain fresh water, the water used is gotten out of a hole about a foot in depth in the sand--and such brackish and hot stuff as filters into such hole, is the hospital water. How sick seamen now fare in regards to dirt, cleanliness, nursing or medical assistance, I do not know, I only speak of what I have seen. My Proposition is this;

The Government to unite the two contracts,the Keeper of the Hospital and Keeper of Ocracoke Light House. Let the airy, cool brick building near the Beacon, intended for the Keeper's residence be occupied by sick seamen. At that spot there are cool shades and tolerable good water. Or shut the inhabitants down if objectionable to have the seaman there. I would occupy it myself and provide as spacious, shaded and well watered accommodations for them more remote from the inhabitants. If I had certainly of a contract that would compensate me, I would spare no pain to deserve my reward. The house at the Beacon is at present of very little service- because inhabited only, a great part of the time, by an old Yellow man, left there to clean and light the Beacon and the keeper's residence, I understand to be 50 or 60 miles distance. He might be transferred to the care of the floating light which is to be placed at Brant Island Shoal, where he would be within a few miles from his family residence and $500 instead of $400, therefore a kindness instead of an injury would be done him by such a transfer.

Let this be done and give me the united contract, and pay me three thousand dollars for the first year, with the understanding that if can live for that price, I will ask no more afterwards, but if I find the sacrifice too serious, I will ask an additional, after the first year of $200 and no more. These contracts cost the government now $1900, and two yea, three good judges, my brother (Dr. Potts) and the others who competed, rated and now rate the compensation, fairly fixed, of the hospital alone $2,000 to $2,500. So that my offer would I conceive be a vast gain to the unfortunate fellows who need this charity.

My family residence should be near the spot, and my daily attention given. A worthy physician, who would not undertake the whole expense of the hospital for less than $2,000 would be employed to give regular attendance. Were I to take the contract, of course it would take effect the day that Dudley's ends, Vis: June, and I would prefer the tenure to be the pleasure of the Present and not more than four years, so as to justify the expense I should have to incur, of course removable for good cause.

I leave here two or three days and would be glad to know before I go.

Joseph B. Hurtow
24th Feb. 1831

On March 14, 1831 Collector Joshua Taylor wrote to S.D.Inghram, Secretary of Treasury, saying that the hospital did have windows and the seamen were well provided for. The hospital had three rooms upstairs and two downstairs and was advantageously situated.

He stated that Dr. Dudley had practiced medicine in Plymouth, North Carolina, for several years before coming to Portsmouth. Furthermore, the inhabitants of Portsmouth patronized him.

The Secretary of Treasury, Louis M. Lane, accepted the testimony of Taylor and extended Dudley's contract.

Dr. Dudley's continuous wealth, power and popularity caused envy among those who could not overpower him. His credibility was again threatened in 1836 by Collector Thomas Robinson. Dudley charged him with slander and was awarded damages.

CASES AT LAW
THE SUPREME COURT
OF
NORTH CAROLINA
VOL.II
SAMUEL DUDLEY vs THOMAS ROBINSON

Calling one a thief or a murderer, in the absence of context or proof to the contrary on the trial, ex vi termini imputs, to him a felony, and therefore an action of slander there lies.

This was the appeal from the judgement of the Superior Court of law of Craven County, at Fall Term, 1841, his Honor Judge Settle presiding. The case made for the Supreme Court is as follows;

Action on the Case. The declaration contained two counts; the first for a libel published in the Washington Whig, a newspaper published in the town of Washington, North Carolina. a copy of which is as follows;

To the Public. It is ascertained and can be proved by the most respectable part of the inhabitants of the island of Portsmouth, that the man, now employed as a physician in the Hospital at that place, has frequently left it on his own private business, with several sick men in the Hospital without any medical aid whatever; and three or four have died in his absence. At one time he was gone fifteen or twenty days, and no physician left in his stead. We feel for our fellow beings, who have to be left in such a place without any assistance and also for ourselves; for during the month of January last, the small pox broke out in the hospital, which joins the dwelling of the pretended doctor. The disease being in the center of the inhabitants, they of course protested against it remaining among them, and requested the aforesaid doctor to remove the patients to Shell Castle, which he refused to do, until he was threatened to have them removed by violence. After they were removed there, four died out of ten without any medical aid; the present physician refusing to visit the patients.

The collector then sent to Beaufort for a physician, but could not obtain one, and in this deplorable situation these unfortunate people were left without medical assistance.

THOMAS ROBINSON
Portsmouth, Feb. 25th, 1836

The second count charged that the defendant spoke and published of and concerning the plaintiff, in the presence of several citizens in a public store, the following words: "Doctor Dudley (meaning the plaintiff) is a thief and murderer." The pleas were, general issue, justification and statute of limitations.

To sustain the first count in the declaration, evidence was offered, proving that the defendant brought the libel aforesaid in manuscript to the office of the Whig, and caused and procured the publication thereof in the Whig; and that the said paper had a considerable circulation, there being at that time of the publication between two and three hundred subscribers. It also appeared in evidence that the plaintiff was at and before the time of the said publication the Hospital physician of the United States at the Hospital on Portsmouth Island in this State. Under the second count it was proved that the defendant, within six months before the action, in a public store at Portsmouth, in presence and hearing of several persons, said "Doctor Dudley is a rogue, liar, thief and murderer." His honor held and instructed the jury that each of the words "thief and murderer" was accountable. There was no colloquium proved of any particular larceny nor did it appear that any particular individual was referred to, as having been murdered by the plaintiff. No exception was taken to the first count; but objection was made on the trial, as to the words "thief and murder" not being accountable. The jury found a verdict on all issues for the plaintiff on both counts, and assessed his damages at $200. A motion for a new trial was made, on the ground that the words "thief and murderer," charged in the second count, were not accountable. A new trial was refused, and the defendant appealed.

SHIPS OWNED BY DR. SAMUEL DUDLEY
CERTIFICATE OF ENROLLMENT
PORT OCRACOKE

CONVOY   OWNER; SAMUEL DUDLEY, WALLIS
              STYRON & THOMAS W. STYRON, all of
              Portsmouth, WALLACE W. STYRON,
              Master. Built Saybrook, Conn.1832. 1 deck,
              2 mast, 65 ft. long, 21 ft. wide,10 ft. deep,
              75 ton, square stern, scroll Head. Change of
              property and district. Reg. Ocracoke 1835.
              SCHOONER.

MELISSA   OWNER; SAMUEL DUDLEY of
              Portsmouth, JASPER MARTIN Master. Built
              at Currituck Court House in 1829, Reg.
              Ocracoke 1835, 1 deck, 2 mast, length 70 ft.
              8 in., 17 ft. 8 in. wide. 7 ft. 8 in.deep, square
              stern. SCHOONER.

WM R.   OWNERS; SAMUEL DUDLEY of
SMITH   Portsmouth and RUSSEL of New Bern, 1
              deck, 2 mast, 67 ft. long, 17 ft. wide, 5 ft.
              deep, 51 ton, square stern, Billet Head. 1837.

ERIE   OWNER; SAMUEL DUDLEY, of
              Portsmouth, SIMPSON Master. 56 ft. long.
              Property change. (no date).

TWO WAY   OWNER; SAMUEL DUDLEY, of Portsmouth
              ALEXANDRA B. SILVERTON, Master.
              Built New Jersey 1843, 64 ft. long, 1853.

SURRENDER*
CERTIFICATE OF ENROLLMENT

1824
Aug. 1   ALERT - SAMUEL DUDLEY-OWNER and
                 MASTER, new vessel, surrendered Elizabeth
                 City 4 Feb. 1833, property change.

1835
Mar. 16   CONVOY - SAMUEL DUDLEY-OWNER,
                 WALLACE STYRON, MASTER. District
                 change 16 Feb.1833 N.Y., 74 ton surrendered
                 Ocracoke 16 Mar.1836.

Jun. 6   MELISSA - SAMUEL DUDLEY,
                 I. GASKILL, new owners, 42 ton 1839.

Jul. 28   ZILPHA - SAMUEL DUDLEY - OWNER,
                 B. STYRON-MASTER NEW VESSEL,
                 60 TON.

1836
Apr.   W.P. SMITH - SAMUEL DUDLEY -
                 OWNER, 13 Nov. 1835 Plymouth, 51 ton.
                 25 Jan. 1837, Ocracoke, surrendered.

*Certificate of Enrollment was surrendered when vessel was
sold, lost or for any reason no longer in operation.

Samuel Dudley was born in 1790 somewhere in the state of New Hampshire.(Census records 1850 - 1860) He married Susan Salsberry of Princess Ann County, Virginia about 1830, just about the time he moved to Portsmouth. She would have been only 16 years old.

The 1830 census list;

Samuel Dudley as head of house. In house with him are 1 male 20/30 and one female 15/20 years of age. The female would have been his wife. (Determined by following census records for the next thirty years). The male 20\30 could have been a brother or another employee of the marine hospital. Samuel would have been forty years of age, which means it would have been possible that he was married before and the other male could have been a son by the previous marriage.

1840 census

Samuel was listed as head of house, the other male was no longer in house. 1 female 20/30 (Susan), 1 male 5/10 (Augustus), 1 female 15/20, 1 female 0/5.

Augustus Dudley's Bible records state that he was born March 9th, 1883, which would make him the male listed as 5/ 10. The female 15/20 is unexplained. The female 0/5 would have been their 2nd child. She must have died very young for she is not listed in the next census. There could have been other children that died as infants since there is a span of about seven years before another child is recorded.

1850 census

			Born
SAMUEL DUDLEY	60 male	Physician	New Hampshire
SUSAN D.	36 female		
AUGUSTUS	19 male		
ALMERIA	8 female		
SUSAN	5 female		
JOHN W.	3 male		
JOHN HOOVER	18 male	Mariner*	
THOMAS WILLIAMS	16 male	Mariner*	England

* These could have been patients of his or crewmen from one of his ships.

1860 census

SAMUEL DUDLEY	70 male	Doctor - New Hampshire
SUSAN	46 female	
AUGUSTUS	28 male	Merchant
ALMEDIA (ALMERIA)	17 female	
SUSAN	15 female	
JOHN	13 male	
SAMUEL	3 male	

     Samuel died in 1877 and his remains buried on Portsmouth Island, near the old home place. Island lore is that he was buried in a brick vault with a cement slab covering the site. As it is custom on the outer banks he was buried with his head to the west and his feet to the east. When his remains were dug up in the 1920's his head was to the east, suggesting that he may not have been dead when buried or that there was something mysterious about his burial. All that remain today are the bricks that border the burial site.

INVENTORY OF THE ESTATE OF SAMUEL DUDLEY
DECEASED

mule & cart	$25.00
10 bee hives	10.00
1 bed, bolster and 2 pillows	5.00
1 blanket & 1 quilt	.75
1 bed stead	.75
1 chest	.25
1/2 doz chairs	.50
1 lot crockery ware	.75
1 carpet & table	.75
1 pot, spider and tea kettle	1.00
1 cupboard	.75
1 gun & sword & c	1.00
1 lot of jugs and jars	.75
1 lot truck	.75
1 lot hoes	.50
1 lot baskets	.50
1 plow and traces	1.00
1 cannon ??	2.25
3 axes	.75
1 brass kettle	.25
2 steel traps & 1 half bushel measure	1.25

Balance due from Shade Bryan   5.50

                                                 $60.00
4 hogs ---8.00

                                                 $68.00

In 1860 Samuel Dudley was listed a having the following slaves:

1	BLACK	MALE	AGE	63 YEARS
1	MULATTO	FEMALE	AGE	56 YEARS
1	MULATTO	FEMALE	AGE	21 YEARS
1	BLACK	FEMALE	AGE	17 YEARS
1	BLACK	MALE	AGE	4 YEARS
1	BLACK	FEMALE	AGE	1 YEAR

Dr. Dudley was a legion in his time and remains one today. His memory has been carried on through every generation on Portsmouth and Ocracoke Islands.

Samuel's son Augustus Dudley married Maltilda Swindell on June 14, 1866 and lived in Hyde County. He died in 1912 and is buried in the Amity Church Cemetery, Highway 264, Lake Landing, NC. He was a resident of Portsmouth during the Civil War and detailed accounts of his roll in the war are covered in Chapter 10, CIVIL WAR.

In Augustus Dudley's Bible in the possession of Mrs. Blanch Dudley of Engelhard, NC is the following entry; April 15th 1933, R.A. DUDLEY oldest of Dudley family now alive - sixty six years old today. Offspring of DOCTOR SAMUEL DUDLEY of New Hampshire and SUSAN SALSBERRY his wife of Virginia. GRANDPARENTS.

Samuel's son John W. Dudley and wife Susan were living at Portsmouth in 1880. They had Georgie A. age 6, Fanny age 4 and Samuel age 2. The family moved to Washington, NC, where he died in 1914.

The following information comes from his death certificate.
NAME: Capt. Jno W. DUDLEY (W), Married, Steam boat Capt.
BORN: 11 Mar. 1847 - Portsmouth, NC
DIED: 16 Feb. 1914 - Washington, NC
BURIED: 17 Feb. 1914 - Oakdale Cemetery, Washington, NC
FATHER: Samuel DUDLEY - New Hampton
MOTHER: Susan SALISBURY - Princess Ann County, Va.
INFORMANT: A.S. FULFORD
CAUSE OF DEATH: Apoplexy with lagrippe

Dr. Samuel Dudley's great grandchildren, Bill Dudley and his sister, Mary; grandchildren of August Dudley, visit Portsmouth Island for the first time in July 1994.

CHAPTER 4

JOHN WALLACE, "GOVERNOR OF SHELL CASTLE"

JOHN WALLACE was born in 1758, the son of DAVID WALLACE of Portsmouth Island. His wife was REBECCA (last name unknown, no marriage records found in this state.) He was the mastermind of the Blount and Wallace enterprise at Shell Castle, and was called "The Governor of Shell Castle". It was he who ruled over the island and all activities there. In May of 1794 he was appointed agent for employing workmen and supplying materials for the fortification at Beacon Island.

On 29 Nov. 1797 Wallace and Blount sold part of Shell Castle to the government which then constructed a wooden lighthouse there.

Found in an old unnumbered deed book, at the Carteret County Register of Deeds, Beaufort, N. C. is the following deed:

Page 205   29 November 1797

JOHN GRAY BLOUNT of Washington, NC and John Wallace of Shell Castle, NC to the United States of America----for $200 Land for the purpose expressed in an Act of Assembly of the state of North Carolina, passed at Raleigh in the year 1794 entitled an Act for ceding to the United States the Jurisdiction of certain land on Shell Castle Island:

  In the Harbor of Ocracoke a certain lott on Shell Castle at the Eastermost end thereof and to run along the rock to the Westward with Wallace Channel, seventy feet, then to beginning. With the stipulation that the U.S. shall not permit goods to be stored, a Tavern to be kept, to be no retailed or Merchandise to be carried on, on sd lott, or suffer any person to reside on or make that a stand from which they may either pilot or lighter vessels.

                                                    J.G. Blount
                                                    John Wallace

Wallace was active in all fields of Shipping and commerce. The *JOHN GRAY BLOUNT PAPERS* published by the Division of Archives and History, are packed with information on Shell Castle. Some of these letters are included here to document the activities at the time. The stress of managing such an extensive empire evidently drove Wallace to drink and possibly to an early grave. He was only 52 at the time of his death. A letter from one William Smith, storekeeper at Shell Castle to John Gray Blount complains of Wallace having hands in the till and of being drunk "four times a week." It was because of Shell Castle that Portsmouth grew so rapidly. Most of the employees lived either on Portsmouth, or Sheep Island, on the south end of Portsmouth Island.

John Wallace made his home on Shell Castle, though he too may have built a home on Sheep Island. In a letter to John Gray Blount, dated Sept. 22, 1792 he writes, "The bricks I want for the Old wench a chimney to our New House ashore, certainly before it gets too cold."

John Wallace's father David Wallace and brother David Jr. both lived in the village of Portsmouth. A 1797 map shows both residences, and uses them as a navigation point in crossing the bar at Ocracoke Inlet. David Wallace was one of the wealthiest men on Portsmouth. The 1800 census shows he owned 26 slaves. He was employed by the government to buoy and mark the shoals and channels at Ocracoke Inlet and Pamlico Sound. David Jr. worked for brother John Wallace at

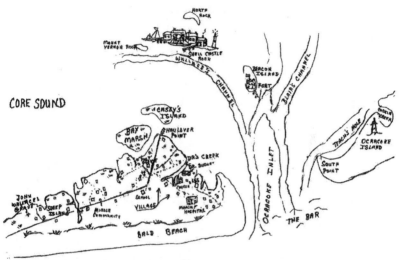

PAMLICO SOUND

CORE SOUND

PORTSMOUTH ISLAND

ATLANTIC OCEAN

A MAP OF
PORTSMOUTH ISLAND,
SHELL CASTLE ROCK,
BEACON ISLAND
AND OCRACOKE INLET
1790-1815

by Ellen F. Cloud

Shell Castle, as a mate on the "Beaver" (a boat used for lightering). He also worked with the fishing fleet, in season and was busy "wrecking" after storms cast away ships on the coast. He later became Captain of one of the Revenue Cutters stationed at Ocracoke. By 1827 David Wallace Jr. was living at Ocracoke.

Records show that John and Rebecca Wallace did not let their children mingle with other residents of the area but instead, kept them close within the family circle, for their children married children of John's brother David Wallace.

It has been said of the Chadwick family in Carteret County, that they married within the family in order to keep their land and acquire larger tracts by joining the property of the families. This might be the case with the Wallaces. It is not known, but it is certain that there were many intermarriages. Listed below are the children of John and David Wallace, and it appears to be the pattern throughout the Wallace family.

JOHN WALLACE and REBECCA had issue;

*LOUISA WALLACE	m.	CAPT. JAMES WALLACE
*THOMAS B. WALLACE	m.	dau. of DAVID WALLACE*
*PATSY WALLACE	m.	WILLIAM WALLACE
HORATIO WALLACE	m.	NANCY WALLACE
ELIZABETH WALLACE	m.	WALLACE WHITEHURST

DAVID WALLACE, brother of JOHN WALLACE, wife Hannah, had the following children;

*JAMES WALLACE	m.	LOUISA WALLACE
MARY WALLACE	m.	ALEXANDER HENDERSON
*WILLIAM H. WALLACE	m.	PATSY WALLACE
HARRIET WALLACE	m.	STEVEN FIELDS
FRANCES N. WALLACE	m.	ISRAEL SHELDEN
*DAUGHTER	m.	THOMAS B. WALLACE*

THE BLOUNT PAPERS

Pg. 288, VOL 2
1790 -1795

JOHN WALLACE to JOHN GRAY BLOUNT

                    SHELL CASTLE,JULY 17TH 1793
Dear Sir

        by Reubin Wallace I send to you for 6 or 8 thousand of
22 inch Shingles 12 or 15 hundred of boards for to finish the
weather boarding and plank Enough to Lay both the floors as
we have not more than will make doors and windows. wee
have now two Carpenters at work if I can not get Plank and
Shingles I must be obliged to discharge them before the house
is finished, they have not more work than will last till
Sunday.
        Please to send a barrel of good sugar for ours is just
out, three barrels of Tar, two Gallons of Varnish, a barrel of
Pork and some bacon and apples if to be had.
        4 of the Negroes that I hired from Core Sound stold
our Boat on Saturday night and ran away. I have been from
then till now after them have ketch one of them and got the
Boat again---the other three Nat Pinchkam is after and I think
well get them this week; I am obliged to put Will in a flat
to bring shells; the Beaver we have just cleaned and gives
her a bottom of Rosin and whale oil which I think is best
Ever was put on a vessel bottom. 4 gallons of oil and one Bl
of Rosin leans her twice, about the 26th I will come in the
Beaver about the Staks. No nuse hear from any place nor
nothing to do but work, your order on Makey he would not
pay. flint I settled and will bring your money when I come, any
thing that you know that I have not wrote you Enquire of
Reubin and pleas to Dispatch him as soon as possible. I Send
you a mess of Coccles also to Major Blount his home spun for
Trousers.   .   all well here
                                          John Wallace

P.S. I sent to bay River for Shingles and none to be had at that
place.   JW

Pg. 404
THOMAS BLOUNT TO JOHN GRAY BLOUNT

PHILA. 6TH June 1794

Dear Sir;
The head of the TOOLEY will be finished in 14 days I hope in
time to go home by the vessel you are sending or have sent
but it will be a female one & therefore the Vessel whether
Ship or Brig should have a female name & I have half a mind
to propose that it should be REBECCA..
Yours & C.
THOMAS BLOUNT

Pg 139 VOL III
JOHN WALLACE TO JOHN GRAY BLOUNT

SHELL CASTLE
April 8th, 1797

I send you the dementions of the STORE, and am anxious to
hear from you to hear about my corn, as I am all most out,
and my FATHER is quite out. No news here. We are all well
at the CASTLE, BRITT is in the roads tells WISE that I sent
this morning to carry him out, that he is two sick to go to
sea today, but I am afraid he is afraid to go.
In Hastes, Yours
JOHN WALLACE.

ENCLOSURES,
9ft. from floor to floor
20 ft. in width
3 ft. 8 in from plate to plate
40 ft in length.
14 1/2 ft. rafters
14 1/2 ft. wind beams
Plates 9 1/2 in by 4

Pg. 392
June 30, 1800

Dr. Sir.

Yours by Capt. How came to hand, the "CALEB" I had sold before, it come to hand for $1150. to be paid at Perquimous in Corn and white OAK HOGSHEAD STAVES & heading Day Corn at $2 oer Bll Staves & heading at $16 pr m. The "BEAVER" is now gone after the pay for the "CALEB". I am half done Logging the CASTLE, and at work on the other half, but have not trees enough to finish I have them cut in the Woods but cannot git wheels stout enough to draw them down, do if you have not sent a pair before this comes to hand do it, or write me and I must send for a pair some where else. I am the Busiest that I ever was in my life, 40 to 45 in my family and employees. CAPT. HOW sails for LONG SHOAL that moment the wind will let up. We are all well at the CASTLE with respect to you and family. No news here, if you any please write.

Yours & c
JOHN WALLACE

Pg 382-3 VOL III
JOHN WALLACE TO JOHN GRAY BLOUNT

I have purchased the "FLOUNDER" for us of ROSS, for Eight hundred & thirty two dollars & a half for her boat & the Old Boat, which is to be paid in lighterage & Pilotage, part of which is already paid; She comes up now for the first business to bring down TAYLORS HOUSE, or whatever part she can bring and the rest she will bring at some other time or some other lighter. HOW continues in her as he did with CAPT. ROSS. If we have not a plenty of Lightering for her to do after this business we will put her to carrying Shingles to the Federal City, Baltimore, or elsewhere, and bringing Stone Ballast back. She will carry two hundred thousand of your longer shingles at least. You with CAPT. ROSS will do what is necessary with her papers at Washington. I have this thirty days past generally been from home after our logs. I have not got one hundred down at the CASTLE and the other hundred is cart ing down, The quantity will complete our business.I have a thousand other things to write but have no time. But must request of you to inform me, near what time you can be down, and think (as we have got to much business on hand) if the office (as piaza) will do for you, and we have a good kitchen that will serve for all cooking and we can have our writing and all business done in MAYO'S HOUSE or the GENERALS on the wharf.

I expect the "CALEB" every day, but have not heard from her, should she not come in the course of a fornight, or three weeks, I will write to you to have her insured, & furnish you with bill of lading to the amount of property, should she come with a load of salt. I shall want to land it here, as CAPT. TAYLOR says he will permit it be done & secure the duties. We are all well at the CASTLE with respect to you and family & friends and remain

Dear Sir Your Most Obedt.
Hol Servant
JOHN Wallace

JOHN WALLACE TO JOHN GRAY BLOUNT
DR SIR,

Your letter of the 29th May come to hand by Capt. How, Capt Fletcher has not returned this way, I suppose came in at New Inlet and gone to Long Shoal, I now send the "Flounder" up to load with shingles..

I have now our work at the East end of the CASTLE (warehouse) almost logged up and am going tomorrow for my other logs to finish that and log up as much more at the other end of the CASTLE all which logs I have now down at the water, which work I expect to have completed in the course of Six weeks if the weather permits, which just makes the CASTLE.

I have a great many men employed, which takes all the money I can get hold of for their provision & pay their wages. I have had luck in getting money from all quarters, the "CALEB" fell greatly short by getting her cargo damaged.. I am obliged to go after the logs and attend to them myself which keeps me great part of my time from home, but I hope by the end of next week to get them, when I expect to continue at home and carry on the work with as much dispatch as possible. Tom Blount has been very sick but is now on the recovery all the rest of the family on the CASTLE are all well as the rest of your friends at this place. With compliments to Mrs. Blount & family.

JOHN WALLACE

JOHN GRAY BLOUNT TO JOHN WALLACE

WASHINGTON JULY 11,1810

JOHN WALLACE ESQ.

DR. SIR

As we are both advanced in years and have each a family for which we ought to make some arrangements. And as we hold a Property jointly which we may wish to use for that purpose and have a long standing Acct. which none but ourselves can settle and perhaps even ourselves with some difficulty I have for some time past had it in contemplation to make you the following offer; to wit to draw a Line across the Castle at the East end of the old or large Ware House straight to the end of the House and give you the choice of ends of the Castle & Rock and I have no doubt you will choose the West end which I would prefer by 1000 $ but as your House is on it shall not object to you taking it. To let Persons be appointed to divide all the other Lands and Property owned by us jointly by reducing the same and drawing lots. And appointing a person to collect all the outstanding Debts & pay all the Debts due and then divide the balance or pay equally the balance if the Sum due us will not pay. Say nothing of any acct. either of us have for anything whatever, as you have a claim for annual wages & I have a claim for Negro hire & I suppose you have no Account of house expense a part of which has from time to time been supplied from joint property no doubt, and of course the going into those Accts would occasion much difficulty.

If you accede to this mode please have a List made of all joint Property and sign it. make to me a deed to my half the Castle and Rock and appoint the Person in Writing to divide the other joint property and this letter shall oblige me to do the same to you.

The Part of the Town to the time of division to be joint property as well as the profits of the undivided Hands until divided.

I hope this offer will be taken in the same friendly disposition in which it is offered.

And am with sincere esteem
your most Obed
JG BLOUNT

Addressed: JOHN WALLACE, ESQ
SHELL CASTLE

NOTE; JOHN WALLACE died on July 22,1810---JOHN GRAY BLOUNTS letter must have been prompted by news that his partner was in poor health. The property was not divided before he died.

John Wallace and his wife were buried on Sheep Island. A concrete slab covers the "Governor's" grave with an epitaph written in Old English.

Here are Deposited
the Remains of
Captain John Wallace
Governor of Shell Castle
who departed this life
July 22, 1810
age 52 years and 6 months
Shell Castle Mourns Your pride is in the dust
Your boast, your glories in the dreary grave.
Your sun is set ne'er to Illume again
This sweet asylum from th' Atlantic Wave.
He's here beneath this monumental stone
This awful gloom anid the silent dead.
Thy founder lies whose sainted soul we laid
To heaven's high mansion has its journey sped.
Mourn charity benevolence bewail
Kind hospitality his lot deplore.
And own with one unanimous accaim
Misfortune's sons will view his like no more.

Most of John Wallace's heirs were married and had their homes on Sheep Island at the time his estate was settled.

It was a common practice for widows to have their minor sons bound to influential persons to learn a trade and in order to lesson the burden of support for herself. Sometimes boys in trouble with the law were bound to someone for a period as punishment for a crime instead of imprisonment.

Beaufort County Court Minutes, June Term 1812-- "Ordered that Thomas Blount Wallace orphan of John Wallace Esq. of Shell castle--now of the age of (left blank) be bound to Lewis Leroy until he reaches the age of 21 to learn the trade of Merchant--. (Mr. Leroy was a Merchant in Washington, NC).

In 1793 a Mrs. Clifton had a son about 16 years old, who she was "anxious to dispose of in some manner--" requests that he be bound to J.B. Blount to work at Shell Castle.

Rebecca Wallace, widow of John Wallace chose to remain on Shell castle after her husband died and attempted to make life miserable for all around her. It seems that no one on the Island could live in peace because of her and she was eventually removed from the Island. The following letter is a good example of the kind of neighbor she was.

SOLOMON M. JOSEPH to JOHN GRAY BLOUNT
SHELL CASTLE MARCH 7, 1811
JOHN G. BLOUNT ESQ.

Sir,
It seems the avaricious, and over grasping woman, who is daily pleading distress and poverty, and her lonely distress'd situation, will not leave me undisturbed, on this small piece of ground which I hold at so high a price,--she being without the least feeling of gratitude to any person but herself, I have no doubt she must disturb you among the rest... It is only a power

which Mrs. Wallace wishes to monopolys, that others may humble to her for a few greens,..after Mrs. Joseph has been at the trouble of sewing seed..Yesterday Mrs. Wallace called on Mrs. Joseph and told her she could not think of her having a garden without pay as she was a poor woman and had a Large family to Support..It is only envy, there is no doubt Mrs. Wallace has and knows how to take care of herself without the production of the Garden..

CHAPTER 5

PILOTS AT OCRACOKE INLET

In 1715 an Act was passed to settle and maintain Pilots at Ocracoke Inlet, "it being the only port with sufficient dept of water for ships of Burden between Topsail and the Virginia Capes." These men, the pilots were the first to establish residence at Ocracoke and Portsmouth. At first they did not own the land on which they lived, but were squatters and had only huts to protect them from the elements of the weather.

They kept to themselves and avoided the outside world. Their main interest was to keep Ocracoke Inlet open and safe for the shipping through the Inlet. They were suspicious of outsiders and rightly so, since every day they dealt with pirates, enemy ships, smugglers and invaders. These pilots were hard and rough men and often called "Wild and Barbarous," "Unwashed Barbarians," "Slovenly Brutes," "Ignorant Beast," and worse.

Through the years the Pilots married daughters of the first landholders, thence acquiring land and building homes. These pilots were to become the ancestors of the people of that part of the Outer Banks, divided by Ocracoke Inlet, known as Ocracoke and Portsmouth Islands.

Most of the people who first saw the Islands were eager to move on, the fear of Coastal Storms and the shallow sounds made settlement difficult. The greatest fear was of the Pirates who often used the area to relax and party.

Because pilots and pirates were the main inhabitants, Ocracoke grew very slowly, while Portsmouth grew more rapidly, but even Portsmouth was avoided by all except those employed in the shipping business.

Only men with their knowledge of the changing channels and shoals of the dangerous and treacherous Inlet, men said to have "salt in their blood" could make a living from the sea and cope with all the changes.

In 1760 a Bill was passed to lay off 50 acres of land on Ocracoke Island for the use of the Public, where Pilots might reside and have room to pull up their boats for repair. Just a few years later, the pilots requested the government to lay off 25 acres for the same purpose saying that the land before assigned has since "washed away and gone."

In 1766 an Act for Facilitating the Navigation of Port Bath, Port Roanoke, and Port Beaufort was established and set forth the following regulations;

Commissioners were appointed to contract with proper persons to examine, from time to time, the situation of the Swash and keep the channels leading from Ocracoke Bar, to Port Bath, Edenton and New Bern well and sufficiently staked out, and to erect Beacons at Ocracoke, Beacon Island, and Core Bank ..for the safety of vessels.

Said Commissioners shall have the authority to examine Pilots touching their qualifications. In order to obtain his warrant to Pilot Vessels in all or any ports.----in case any person shall pretend to pilot or take charge of any vessel or ship without having passed an Examination and obtained a warrant for so doing and also posted bond of One Hundred Pounds, with two good securities. And be it Enacted, that there shall be paid to every Pilot who shall take charge of any Ship or vessel, the following Pilotage; that is to say;

For every ship or vessel from the outside of the Bar of Ocracoke into Beacon Island Road. Two Shillings, Proclamation Money, per Foot for every vessel that draws Nine feet of water, or less; and for every vessel drawing Ten Feet and upwards, Three Shillings per foot.

And when any vessel whatsoever shall make a Signal for a Pilot or not, any Pilot who shall go over the Bar aforesaid to Pilot such vessel into Port, and offer his service for that purpose, shall be entitled, although the Master of such vessel shall refuse to employ him, to half the fees which he would be in entitled to if he had taken charge, and piloted such vessel over the Bar, and the Master shall be obliged to pay the same.

In 1773 George Bell. John Bragg, Adam Gaskill, Richard Wade, William Styron and Simon Hall, all pilots at Ocracoke Inlet sent a petition to the Governor complaining that a number of negroes, some of whom were slaves brought down by their owners and also other freemen of color were trying to take over their jobs, and seriously affecting their business.

This problem was soon taken care of and the pilots continued to serve the needs of the shipping industry as well as risk their lives protecting the coast during times of war. They were the first to come face to face with the enemy at the beginning of war, for one of the first goals of the enemy (whoever it might be) was to blockade the inlet, thus making threats on the business of piloting.

With the coming of the steam engine, shipping through Ocracoke Inlet was on a rapid decline. The cargo no longer had to be transported by water, across Pamlico Sound and up the rivers. Ships unloaded at other ports where the cargo would be delivered by train which was much faster and less costly. With the decrees in shipping through the inlet came the decrease in the need for pilots. By the 1900 census there were no pilots listed at Portsmouth and only two at Ocracoke.

Pilot's Branch.

To all People to whom these Presents shall come..

KNOW Ye, That we *John R Blount   Joseph*
.... Water Bond William Right
....   Esquires, Commissioners
of the Navigation of Port Roanoke, in the State of North-
Carolina, having examined *Christopher Oneal, Jun.*
touching his abilities as a Pilot, and it being also certified
unto us that he is a good orderly and peaceable citizen of
this State, and that he is a proper and well qualified person
to be and act as a Pilot for the Bar of Occacock, and the
several ports of Bath, Roanoke, Currituck, and Beaufort :.

THESE *are therefore to make known,* That the said
                                        — is empowered to be and act as
a Pilot for the Bar of Occacock, and the several Ports of
Bath, Roanoke, Currituck and Beaufort, aforesaid, and that
he is entitled to all the rights, privileges and emoluments
thereunto belonging.

GIVEN *under our Hands and Seals, this* 30 *day of* July 1824.
one thousand eight hundred and 24 *and in the*
year of American Independence. XX VIII

Joseph ....

W. Right   *Nat Bond*

Pilot License of Author's Great Great Great Grandfather,
Christopher O'Neal, Jr. (b. 1791 - d. 1860)

PILOT'S BRANCH.

To all People to whom these presents shall come :

Know ye —that we, *Wallace W Simpson Benjamin oneal Joseph Roberts Francis Williams sen*

Esquires, Commissioners of Navigation for the Port of *Ocracoke*

In the State of North Carolina, having received from the Board of Branch Pilots, appointed by an act of the General Assembly, passed in the year of our Lord one thousand eight hundred and twenty-four, a certificate of

Christopher oneal

being qualified to act as a Pilot for the Bar and Swashes, and he the the said, *Christopher oneal*

having satisfied us of his being qualified to Pilot in the sounds of Pamlico and Albemarle to the Ports of Edenton Elizabeth City and Plymouth :—These are to make known that he said

Christopher oneal

is empowered to be and act as a Pilot for the Bar of Ocracoke and the Swashes, and from thence to the Ports of Edenton, Elizabeth City and Plymouth ; And that he is entitled to all the rights, privileges and emoluments thereunto belonging

Given under our hands and seals at *Ocracoke March 22 1859*

Wallace W Simpson (Seal)
Benja. G. Aneal (Seal)
Francis Williams (Seal)

Pilot License of Author's Great Great Grandfather,
Christopher O'Neal, Jr. (b. 1826 - d. 1912)

CHAPTER 6

War and Military Activities

Another Island that contributed to the growth of
Portsmouth was Beacon Island, located 2.2 miles northeast of
the village of Portsmouth and 3.8 miles west of the
village of Ocracoke. On this island there have been four
forts, a ship's store, a lighthouse and a hunting club. The island got its name because of two beacons that were located
there which the pilots used to guide ships through Ocracoke
Inlet in the eighteenth century.

It is not always clear when studying records of
Portsmouth which Island is being referred to. As far as the
census records as well as other federal records, Shell
Castle, Beacon Island and Sheep Island are listed under and
included in the Portsmouth district, often with no distinc-
tion noted, with the exception of 1810 census, which list
Portsmouth with 119 males, 106 females and 115 slaves. The
population of Shell Castle was listed as having 18 white
inhabitants and 10 slaves.

THE SPANISH INVASION

In 1747 Spanish privateers took possession of Ocracoke
Inlet, seizing vessels and landing on Ocracoke Island. They
burned vessels, slaughtered and stole cattle, hogs and sheep
and killed several inhabitants. The Islanders complained to
the governor who promised to erect a fort there for their
protection as well as the protection of the commerce through
the Inlet.

From the Colonial Records Vol III comes the following information;

The Military aspect of government in royal North Carolina was represented chiefly by the militia, an institution existing in the province from the dawn of the proprietary era. With the outbreak of hostilities between Britan and Spain in 1739, a conflict that widened in 1744 to include France as an enemy, North Carolina for the first time became a direct participant in a major war for empire. Indicative of the province's expanding role as one of the King's dominions was the passage of an act in 1740 permitting the governor to send militia to the assistance of Virginia and South Carolina if those colonies were invaded. No militiamen were in fact sent, but four companies of 100 men each were recruited in the northern counties and one from the Cape Fear region. Early in the war Spanish privateers began to infest the coast and in June and July 1741, crossed Ocracoke Bar and staged several landings, seizing "Hoggs and Black Cattle."

A thoroughly alarmed Governor Johnson requested naval assistance from South Carolina and Virginia and begged the Admiralty in London for a warship to cruise between Cape Fear and Cape Hatteras, noting that province was devoid of naval protection, ordnance, ammunition, or fortifications.

Governor Johnston at Edenton writes to The Lords of the Board of Trade;

"In 1747 several small Sloops came creeping along the shore from St Augustine full of armed men mostly Mulattoes and negroes, they landed at Ocracoke, Core Sound, Bear Inlet and Cape Fear, where they killed several of his Majesty's subjects, burned some ships and several small vessels, carried off some negroes and slaughtered a vast number of Black Cattle and Hogs, this continued all the summer of 1747. The enraged people exclaiming there would be no safety for them without forts.

Four Forts should be built, two large ones, one at Ocracoke, the other at Cape Fear and two smaller ones,one at Core Sound, the other at Bear Island."
Edenton, April 4th 1749   G. Johnston

Seven years later* a fort was finally being built. From New Bern, on 10th July 1756 Governor Dobbs writes to the Earls of London;

"Last summer I went down with the Commissioners to fix upon a place to build a Fort near Ocracoke Bar, and agreed to erect a Battery with two faces on Core Banks at Portsmouth, where one face would play upon all Harbor. As I found a Violent storm about five years ago had carried away Beacon Island, which was near two miles long, and all Banks here in time may be lyable to the like, I thought it more prudent to erect a large battery upon piles, and rise it 5 ft. above the usual spring tides than to risk the building and Fort, and to build a strong House to defend the Battery. I went down about a forthnight ago to see how far they had proceeded and I find the whole almost piled and filled, and the house ready to be framed, and as I propose it to be a fascine Battery, it will soon be ready. We shall want 8 eighteen pounders for the face next to the Bar and 12 Twelve pounders to defend the harbor with suitable ordnance, stores, and Gunner & C. and about 40 men to defend the House and Battery, which with the seaman in the ships and people of the town may be sufficient against any Privateers which may infest the Coast."

This Fort was Fort Granville.
Charles McNair appointed Captain of the Company stationed there when completed in 1756. In 1758 there were 53 officers and men, in 1762 there were only 25, and in 1764 the garrison was discontinued and the barracks rented.

Joseph Royal, one of the soldiers at Ft. Granville and
John Bragg, a pilot, made an official complaint on 1 Sept.
1759 that Valentine Wade who was a justice-of-peace, and who
also owned a tavern on Portsmouth was allowing and
encouraging "disorderly persons to dance and play at cards
and dice in his house upon the Lord's Day."

Editors note;
  *(I have found several deeds of Portsmouth that mention a
site called "Ballast Stone Hill." As of yet I have been
unable to locate the site and until I heard this interview
with Ms Mattie, I thought I was looking for a pile of ballast
stones. Now I know it will be a location with scattered
stones marking grave sites. Ms. Mattie tells that she owned
the property and when her uncle was trying to dig a grave for
his deceased wife, he was unable to do so, because everywhere he dug he hit a grave. She states that no one ever knew
there were graves there or how old they were. She goes on to
say that in one grave that was dug up was the remains of a
lady in red. Now we all know that no one, but no one is ever
buried in red, especially in that time, except perhaps a
"Lady of the Night."*
  *This raises the question of the age of these grave
sites? Could they date back to 1759, the days of the tavern?
Were they the persons that were disorderly and dancing? We
know for sure that no wife of the residents of Portsmouth
were behaving this way. There had to be "Ladies of the Night"
on Portsmouth to entertain the seamen that stopped there.)*

THE AMERICAN REVOLUTION

Ocracoke Inlet was one of the most important inlets of the Revolution. The British soon became aware of this, and in 1777 Ocracoke Inlet again was threatened when the British unsuccessfully attempted a blockade. Vessels continued to slip in with supplies and privateers were sneaking out. However the British were successful in capturing some of our vessels. On April 14 the British ship *LILY*, captured the vessel *POLLY*, and a privateer on the same day recaptured the *POLLY* and disarmed the *LILY*. The Pilots at Ocracoke Inlet showed their determination to keep the inlet open for shipping. For three days a group of armed pilots manned five whale boats, proceeded out of the Inlet and captured both vessels and took them to New Bern.

The *POLLY* was a Brig owned by one Robert Neilson, on which he was also Captain. In July of 1776 Neilson had agreed to Import into the Colony a Quantity of Salt, Arms and Ammunition, and gave Bond and sufficient Security to preform the same within eight Months.

The *POLLY* soon left Edenton with a cargo consisting of Sixty thousand pipe and four thousand five hundred Hogshead Staves, three thousand weight of Beeswax and twenty barrels of Turpentine, bound for some of the Ports of the Kingdom of Portugal or Spain. She was on her return voyage with the supplies for the Colony and right on schedule to keep the deadline of eight months, when she was captured by the *LILY*.

Because of the immediate danger to shipping and for protection to the coast a fort was finally built on the Portsmouth side of the Inlet, at Beacon Island. A battery was placed at Ocracoke, The *Caswell* with 145 men commanded by Willis Williams was stationed at the Bar, and on July 12, 1776 Capt. James Anderson writes to the Council of

Safety; "I have made up my Company at Ocracoke----I hope to be capable of guarding against all enemies who may offer to oppose us here."

On July 27,1776 the Commissioners approved the sum of two hundred pounds to be paid to Capt. James Anderson "for the purpose of procuring good and sufficient Guns, drums and Colours for the use of his Independent Company on the Sea Coast in this colony." Anderson also was furnished fifty weight of Gun Powder, and one hundred weight of lead.

On that same day Capt. Anderson was ordered to send an Officer with a sufficient number of men to Cape Hatteras Banks to remove three pieces of iron ordnance over the Banks to Pamlico Sound and to transport the cannon to South Kay on Black Water, and then deliver the same to Virginia. Commissioners were appointed to build and fit out two Gallies for the protection of Ocracoke Inlet.

A letter to Governor Caswell dated Sept. 1777 states that "two English ships, one very large, the other mounting ten or twelve guns had taken several vessels at the bar."

Virginia also knew of the importance of Ocracoke Inlet, and agreed to construct two Row Galleys for North Carolina for the purpose of protecting the inlet. North Carolina had no navy, but began to convert small two masted brigs into warships. There was a joint effort proposed between Virginia and North Carolina to protect the inlet. Virginia was to build the Row Galleys and North Carolina was to fit them out.

The Galleys were to be seventy-five feet long, twenty seven feet wide and ten feet deep amidships. They were to have a quarter deck for the officers and a spar deck for the men. The Galleys were to have twenty-four row ports and six gunports to a side and be armed with sixteen guns, four twenty-four pounders stern and bow chasers, and twelve nine-pounder broadside guns.

Though North Carolina had agreed to rig the vessels, little was ever obtained from this state and Virginia eventually had to supply most of it. Among the items requisitioned for the first galley *CASWELL* which took two years to construct, were; Forty-two bolts of canvas, seventy pounds of twine, three dozen needles, thirty gallons of oil, three dozen sail needles, four cross cut and whip saw files, 1,000 penny nails, 1,000 scupper nails, two large and two small speaking trumpets, six landhorns, one log line, six time glasses, two pump hammers, 1,000 pounds of bacon, one ton of grease, three barrels of flour, 300 ton of lead, three reams of cartridge paper, twenty-four cutlasses, twelve cooper ladles, sixteen cannon cartridge boxes, fifty stands of small arms, and twenty-four powder horns. Also ordered were three compasses, twenty barrels of flour, 100 eighteen-pound shot, eight and three-forths yards broad cloth, thirty-six yards of narrow cloth, ninty-five and a half yards of white linen, seventy-six yards of brown linen, twenty-four pairs of stockings, twenty-five pairs of shoes, twelve hats and three dozen fish hooks. Other purchases included, seventy-two yards of fine cloth, ninety yards of coarse cloth, seventy-five pairs of stockings, seventy one pairs of shoes, 524 yards of white linen, 524 yards of brown linen, forty three hats, fifty blanket and fifty yards of ribbon. ·

The *Caswell* took station at Ocracoke Inlet in the spring of 1778. The other Row Galley to soon join the Caswell at Ocracoke was the *Washington.* Having these vessels on station in the inlet did by no means solve any problems there, for it was next to impossible to find crew members. Most men on the banks had already joined the militia or were privateering. Wages on the privateers were twice that of the Continental or state navies, and the chances to obtain prize money was much greater on the privateers.

When at last the captain did employ a crew for the *Caswell*, he had no success in getting wages for them, and found himself paying the crew with his own money. These conditions led to many crew members deserting to join the privateers.

The *Caswell* remained at its station and took little to no part in protecting the Inlet. The Captain left the ship to travel to New Bern to request leave to visit his family, saying that there was no activity at the Inlet. Meanwhile the pilots and privateers continued to capture ships and supplies. The Governor received letters stating that "The coast is much infested at this time with enemy which are constantly landing men and plundering----------." Never-the-less the *Caswell* laid idle until she was worm eaten and sunk two years after her construction.

A petition was sent to Governor Caswell requesting that the men of the Outer Banks be excused from the draft as they were constantly called upon to defend the coast against British marauders.

THE WAR OF 1812
During the War of 1812 still another fort was erected on Beacon Island. Among the John Gray Blount Papers, is the following letter from J.B. Blount to Governor William Hawkins, dated May 25,1813.

Dear Sir
An express Boat which left Ocacok Bar this morning informs that on Friday last a Schooner with American Colours anchored off the Barr on which a Pilot Boat with four Hands went on board & were informed that the Schooner wanted to come in over the Bar. & still pretended to be Americans & were very liberal in their abuse of the British, but in a short time informed the Pilots that she was the British Schooner the Venus late the Highflying Privateer of Baltimore and that she must be piloted in over the Bar. On the Pilots assuring them

there was not water sufficient for her draft to come in safely they man'd the Pilot Boat with the avowed intention of burning the Revenue Cutter and other Vessels then within the Bar and left the schooner with the signal for a Pilot still flying. In proceeding in to execute their truly British plan they met another Pilot Boat going out to the schooner which they ordered along side of them, and inform'd them they were in want of water on board & requested that they would proceed on board and take on shore a few Casks to fill for them no doubt supposing they would proceed on board and be detained, but they observing the number of armed men and the silence of their Brother Pilots in the first Boat, supposed that all was not right & proceeded no farther towards the schooner than to get off the mark of their muskets & then rowed on shore and give the alarm. On the Officer on the boat observing that, he observed that he wish he had sunk that Boat, that they now must return as she would give the Alarm. They did return on board & in a short time discharged the Pilots observing that they would soon return better prepared to execute their design, & on Sunday last they again return'd off the Bar & took a Sloop which had just gone out. Letters by this boat inform that the Revenue Cutter was not maned or prepared in any way to make residence & that few Inhabitants on both sides of the Inlet are without arms or ammunition but are well disposed not only to resist the attack of the British but to render every assistance to the shipping within the Bar, which are now left wholly unprotected by the sending away the two Gun Boats which were stationed there. From having understood that you intended sending two Companies of Milita to each of the Towns of Edenton,Washington, NewBern and Wilmington, I have taken the liberty of giving you the information this day received and beg leave to offer it is my opinion that one company stationed at Ocacock composed of men accustomed to the water and commanded by a brave and enterprising Captain also acquainted with Ocacock & their Pilot Boats to assist & Supply the Inhabitants there with Arms & Ammunition would afford more security to all the Northern parts on North

Carolina as well as the numerous Vessel now daily arriving there from the Blockade of Virginia than all the Companies that can be stationed in the Towns aforesaid even if the object of them Troops should be to guard against internal Enemies; And as that Subject is before me I will take the liberty of observing that it is my opinion that now the lower counties are supplied with arms if they are judiciously disposed of & a supply of Power & Ball procured there will be nothing to fear from insurrection. And if one Company selected from Hyde or some of the Counties accustomed to the water & commanded by the most active & popular Pilot on Ocacock Island and the US Government can be prevailed on to order back to Ocacock the two Gun Boats lately ordered from there, there will be little danger at Ocacock And without that or the building a Fort on Beacon Island. There is no safety for vessels or other property at Ocacock or its vicinity or even in the Towns of New Bern, Washington or Edenton. The importance of the Subject to myself & my fellow Citizens will I hope justify me in liberty I have in writing you thus freely.

> I am with much respect
> your Excellency most Obedt
> Servt. JGBlount

Before Governor Hawkins could reply, on July 11th the British fleet of nine ships, nineteen barges and 2,000 men, anchored off Ocracoke and made their attack on unarmed Ocracoke and Portsmouth on July 12,1813 seizing 200 cattle, 400 sheep and 1,600 fowl. They broke up all the furniture in houses, ripped open beds, throwing feathers in the wind, and robbed women and children of their clothes. They then broke into the customs office and destroyed all of Singletons law books, outraged by finding nothing more there. The Ocracokers had notified Portsmouth before daybreak that morning that the British were there ready to attack. Customs officer, Thomas Singleton packed all the money and bonds in his office into a trunk and loaded it on the revenue cutter "*Mercury*", ordering Capt. David Wallace to sail quickly to New Bern and sound the alarm. Wallace left immediately but was almost captured by the Britains before he could cross the Swash. They chased him for about ten miles before giving up and turning back. Singleton was taken captive and held two days on ship, until the British were ready to sail, at which time he and four Spaniards were put into a small boat and set adrift in the ocean, and managed to make shore before capsizing in the breakers. Many residents of Portsmouth tried to escape by boat when the British landed, but were ordered back. Old man Richard Casey and his family were among those fleeing. When he failed to return when ordered to do so, he was shot in the chest. Casey survived the incident and the Island at which he was shot was named for him.

After the attack, Col Nathan Tisdale called out the New Bern militia and sent an urgent message for help to Governor Hawkins. Gov. William Hawkins reply to Blount came on July 23,1813, with an apology for his delay and stated that he was strongly "in favor of erecting a fortification on Beacon Island"---"I shall go to Ocracoke perhaps tomorrow for the purpose of satisfying myself by actual observation as to the property and practicability of building a fort on Beacon Island--"

The Pettigrewe Papers Vol 1-1685-1818, mention another incident of great danger. In a letter from Thomas Trotter of Prospect Hill, dated June 1, 1813 to Ebenezer Pettigrewe, are the following words; "We had a letter from Shell Castle the other day, mentioning, that an English Vessel at the Bar sent in his boats to burn the castle and the cutter, but they were prevented by an alarm from a boat discovering them and giving notice."

Another incident with the Pilots occurred on Sept. 26,1813 when a little schooner sat off the bar, to which a pilot boat with four pilots went, thinking she was waiting for a pilot. They took one of the pilots and the boat, made the other three jump overboard in the breakers. When one refused he was pushed overboard. They then sent men ashore at Ocracoke with a white flag to announce officially that Ocracoke and Portsmouth were in a state of blockade. They seized a schooner while there and sent it to Nova Scotia to be sold.

The fort was built, though too late for the protection of the Islands in this war. The cannons for the fort never reached their destination, for they were left on the shore at Shell Castle to rust and rot. The fort was also abandoned and left to decay after the war. The second revenue cutter was lost during the war, the first lost in a storm in 1806. Still another was lost in 1820.

THE CIVIL WAR

Though North Carolina didn't secede from the Union until May 20, 1861, Portsmouth Island was already under Confederate jurisdiction. An Advance Party from the *Washington Grays* had been sent ahead with supplies to prepare for the rest of the troops. They went ashore at night, having to anchor offshore and wade across the shoals with the equipment, in water to their waist. On their first trip ashore they seized the Marine Hospital which was under the Union Jurisdiction, then spent the rest of the night and the next day bringing ashore the supplies, at which time a guard was stationed at each gate and at the door of the building.

On the same day that North Carolina seceded the rest of the *Washington Grays* were sent to Beacon Island along with a procession of steamers and schooners bringing building material, arms and supplies. Upon their arrival the troops began construction of Fort Ocracoke, and despite the hardships involved had the fort almost completed when Brigadier General Gwynn visited the site 10 days later. The General reported to Governor Ellis that the fort now had five guns mounted and twelve more to be mounted within the next few days.

The inlets of the outer banks were most important to the South and fortification began immediately. At Fort Hatteras major work had begun by June 1861, Fort Clark also on Hatteras was ready for service by the end of July and work on Fort Ocracoke on Beacon Island and a fort at Oregon Inlet had begun.

All the hard work in the burning sun and mosquitos was in vain for the fort on Beacon Island was soon to be abandoned without firing a shot. The Rebellion Records give full details of this fort and its destruction by the Union Navy. Copies are included here.

There was also a garrison established on the beach at Portsmouth. One of the companies stationed at Portsmouth, the Greenville Company, known as the *Tar River Boys*, mutinied and things got so bad that the Captain of one of the gunboats was ordered to aim his gun at the house, (the hospital) in which the company was quartered. The commander of the fort on Beacon Island, upon orders aimed two 10 in. cannons at the house. Soon the *Washington Grays* volunteered to go and arrest the mutineers. After some arguments the *Tar River Boys* were convinced to surrender. The mutineers were taken prisoners and a court martial ordered.

In the time of all of this, the *Morris Guards*, *Tar River Boys*, and *Hertford Light* Infantry were ordered to Hatteras to help defend the forts there that felt threatened by the large force of Union ships closing in. By the time they arrived there the Union had already taken the forts and were fast to

VIEW OF OCRACOKE INLET
FROM FORT OCRACOKE ON BEACON ISLAND

capture these troops as they approached.

The bombarding of Hatteras could be heard at Ocracoke and Portsmouth. Fort Ocracoke on Beacon Island was fully manned and would have had no problem keeping off the Yanks, since they would have been unable to enter the inlet in their large ships because of the shoaling. There was a meeting of the officers in charge in the officers quarters and mess hall, (a large house on the island). There was some disagreement on what should be done, but after a while the majority ruled, and it was decided to evacuate. One of the captains seized two schooners from Portsmouth in which they made their get-away leaving the flag behind. A sergeant, engineer and four black workers remained long enough to destroy the guns and all supplies and clothing before taking down the flag and reluctantly leaving for New Bern. On Sept. 5, 1861 *The New York Times* published the following account on the inlets in North Carolina.

External Commerce of the sounds is dependant on three inlets, Hatteras, Ocracoke, and Old Topsail. (now Beaufort Inlet). There is another Inlet called New Inlet or Oregon Inlet which according to U.S. Coast Survey, is almost worthless for navigation. Hatteras Inlet easily admits vessels drawing 15 ft. of water. Ocracoke in mean low water, admits over it's bar vessels drawing 10ft. to 11 ft. It's defenses are believed to be insignificant even compared with those at Hatteras. Old Topsail Inlet at Beaufort, is said to be the best on the North Carolina coast. It is defended by Fort Macon, and, the rebels say, in a very efficient manner. But so they thought of Hatteras. There is but one other Harbor of importance on all the Coast of North Carolina, that of Wilmington--the roads of the Cape Fear River, which empties into the Atlantic 50 or 60 miles down the coast from Beaufort. The navigation of the sounds down to Beaufort is tortuous and tedious and not at all reliable or safe. The closing of Hatteras Inlet therefor inflicts a heavy blow on all the contraband, Commerce and Privateering enterprise in which Virginia and North Carolina have been indulging. Fort Hatteras

is made a naval depot for our blockading fleet, and it is easy to
see that a reasonable force within it, and a war vessel nearby to
beat off landing parties, will make the position impregnable to
the enemy. We shall not wait long, we hope to hear that Ocracoke
Inlet and Fort Macon are under our control.

NY TIMES
Feb.12,1861

The following troop information comes from
"NORTH CAROLINA TROOPS 1861-1865--A ROSTER"
Vol. VI INFANTRY - JORDAN.

COMPANY C,
17TH REGIMENT
N.C. TROOPS

"This company was known as the *TAR RIVER BOYS*
and was formed in Pitt County and enlisted at Greenville on
April 26,1861. THE COMPANY WAS MUSTERED INTO
THE STATE SERVICE AT FORT OCRACOKE ON JULY
13, 1861. This was the Co. that mutinied at Portsmouth just
before receiving orders to go to Hatteras. Most of the Co. was
captured at Hatteras on August 29th,1861 and was confined at
Fort Columbus, New York Harbor. Some of the men were paroled on Dec.17,1861. The remainder were paroled January
25,1862. The parolees were officially exchanged on February 20, 1862, and the company was mustered out of service
on March 20,1862."

A quick summary of the activities of this Company
shows they were not what we would call the Fighting Force of
the South.

Mustered in at Portsmouth where they mutined within
a month, left for Hatteras where they were captured upon
arrival. "ACTIVE SERVICE" six weeks. Five months in prison
and musterd out.

COMPANY D
7TH REGIMENT
N.C. TROOPS

"This Company known as the *HERTFORD LIGHT IN-FANTRY* was composed of Hertford County men and enlisted in Hertford County on May 22,1861. THE COMPANY WAS MUSTERED INTO THE SERVICE AT FORT OCRACOKE ON JULY 13,1861 and was assigned to this regiment as Company D. Most of the company was captured at Fort Hatteras on August 29,1861, and confined at Fort Columbus, New York Harbor until transferred to Fort Waren, Boston Harbor. Some of the men were parolled on Dec. 17,1861; the remainder were paroled on January 25,1862. The parolees were officially mustered out of service on April 5,1862. Some of the men subsequently joined Company C. 17th Regiment N.C. Troops (2nd Organization).

COMPANY H
17TH REGIMENT
N.C. TROOPS

This company known as the *MORRISON GUARDS* was from Washington County and enlisted at Plymouth on May 3,1861. THE COMPANY WAS MUSTERED INTO STATE SERVICE AT BEACON ISLAND ON JUNE 20,1861, and was assigned to this Regiment as Company H. Most of the company was captured at Fort Hatteras on August 29,1861 and was confined at Fort Columbus, New York Harbor. Some of the men were parolled on December 17,1861, the remainder were paroled on January 25,1862. The parolees were officially exchanged on February 20,1862. The company was officially mustered out of the service at Williamson on March 20,1862. Some of the men subsequently joined Company G, 17th Regiment N.C. Troops (2nd Organization).

COMPANY K
17TH REGIMENT
N.C. TROOPS

This Company known as the *CONFEDERATE GUARDS* was from Beaufort County and enlisted at Washington, North Carolina, May 22, 1861. The company left Washington on June 4 for Garysburg where it was mustered into service on June 25, 1861, and assigned to this regiment as Company K. On July 30 the company moved from Garysburg to Raleigh and went into camp near the city. It remained in camp until August 14, when it moved by rail from Raleigh to New Bern and then by boat to Fort Ocracoke on Ocracoke Inlet. After Fort Hatteras fell on August 29, Fort Ocracoke was evacuated. The Company was then stationed at Washington where it remained until October 7, when it moved to Lake Landing, Hyde County. On October 14 it moved to Middleton, Hyde County. The company remained in Hyde County until February, 1862, when it was ordered back to Virginia, where it arrived two days later. On March 5 it left Washington for Suffolk Virginia where it arrived two days later. On March 26,1862, the company was mustered out of service at Suffolk.

THE NEW YORK TIMES, THURSDAY, SEPT. 5, 1861, carried the following account of the prisoners.

THE HATTERAS PRISONERS IN QUARTERS
Yesterday Morning all the prisoners brought to this port on board the *U.S. Frigate Minnesota* were transferred to Fort Wood, on Bedloe's Island and to Castle William, on Governer's Island.
A large number of small boats, containing ladies and gentlemen, surrounded the steamboats *SCTURN* and *S.A. STEVENS* which were employed to carry them to their quarters. They

witnessed the disembarkation in silence, not a word was úttered, the spectators looked upon the prisoners more in sorrow than anger.

The next few pages are found in the Rebellion Records 1860 -1861, Outer Banks History Center, Manteo, N.C.

REBELLION RECORD, 1860-61
Doc. 51
EXPEDITION TO OCRACOKE INLET
Report of Commander Rowan.

UNITED STATES STEAMER *PAWNEE*,
HATTERAS INLET, SEPTEMBER 18,1861

Sir: On Saturday, the 14th inst., I gave a pass to one of the people on Hatteras Island to go to Ocracoke Inlet, for the purpose of bringing his family from Portsmouth. I directed this person to examine the forts on Beacon Island and Portsmouth Island and bring me a true report on the condition of things, the number of guns mounted, if any, and the number dismounted; whether any troops were there, and whether the gun-carriages had all been burned or not, and to report the result to me on his return. On Sunday morning, the 15th inst., the boat came alongside, with the man and his wife and children, in a destitute state. We gave them food, and the surgeon prescribed and furnished medicine for the sick of the family.

The man reported that there were twenty guns in Fort Beacon, and four eight-inch shell guns at Portsmouth; that the guns were spiked and the carriages burned on the 1st. instant, as already reported to you. He also stated that a steamer came to Beacon Island before he left Portsmouth, for the purpose of carrying off the guns. I immediately

UNION SHIPS APPROACHING OCRACOKE INLET

determined to use all the means at my command to prevent the removal of the guns, and forthwith got the steamer *Fanny* alongside to prepare her for this service, and had the launch armed and equipped. I sent a request to Col.Hawkins to give me as many of the Naval Brigade as could be spared, which he cheerfully complied with. When the *Fanny* came along-side, her iron rudder-perch was found so much injured that it would be impossible to send her without repairs, so the forge was gotten up, and the clink of hammers soon succeeded the voices of the crew in their responses to our usual Sunday morning service. I despatched the information to Capt. Chauncy, in the offing, who promptly informed me that he would send in four boats and all his marines. I sent word that I would have great pleasure in cooperating with him as senior officer, and would send him the *Tempest* to tow his boats over Ocracoke bar.

At daybreak on Monday morning the *Fanny* was towed alongside and, her rudder temporarily fitted, the Naval Brigade were taken on board, with four day's provisions and water, and the launch similarly provided for. The expedition, being carefully organized and provided with sledge hammers to break off the truions, and thirty-two pound shot and twenty-seven pound cartridges, to be used in firing one gun against the trunnion of another, left this ship at half-past seven o'clock, the launch commanded by Lieut. Eastman and the expedition under command of Lieut. Maxwell, the executive officer of this ship. I despatched the tug *Tempest* to Capt. Chauncy, she drawing too much water to enter the sound.

At 10 o'clock the *Susquehanna* and tug started for the inlet. On the evening of the same day the tug and *Susquehanna* returned and anchored off Fort Clark. The tug came in next morning, and the pilot informed me that the force from the *Susquehanna* did not enter Ocracoke in consequence of the surf. On the afternoon of the 17th instant I felt much anxiety for our expedition. The *Susquehanna* remained at anchor in the offing, and our force was left to take care of itself. Early this morning the lookout at the masthead gave us the gratifying intelligence that our expedition was in sight, and it reached the ship about eleven o'clock. Lieutenants Maxwell and Eastman performed the service with ability and energy, and bore my thanks. The destruction of the fort is complete, and twenty-two guns disabled. These are all the guns that were there, with the exception of two taken off in the steamboat Albemarle on Sunday. The destruction of the guns was with me a necessity. I therefore hope my course will meet your approval. I enclosed a copy of Lieutenant Maxwell's report, giving all details of this important service, which was performed without any accident of any kind.

I have the honor to be, very respectfully, your obedient servant,

S.C. ROWAN, COMMANDER.
Flag-officer S.C. ROWAN, COMMANDING
ATLANTIC SQUADRON.

REBELLION RECORDS 1860-61
LIEUTENANT MAXWELL'S REPORT

UNITED STATES STEAMER *PAWNEE*
HATTERAS INLET, SEPT. 18

Sir: I have to report that, in compliance with your orders of the 16th, I started for Ocracoke on that day, in the steamer *Fanny*, towing the *Pawnee's* launch. Lieutenant Eastman had charge of the latter, with twenty-two men and six marines from the ship, and twelve-pound howitzer, and I had on board six men and sixty-one soldiers of the Naval

Brigade, under Lieutenants Tillotson and Roe. We arrived within two miles of the fort on Beacon Island at 11 o'clock A.M.,when the *Fanny* grounded. I sent Lieutenant Eastman in the launch to sound for the channel. While he was so occupied, a sailboat with two men put off from Portsmouth to cross the sound. A shot from the *Fanny* brought them alongside, and they piloted us to within an hundred yards of the fort. It is called Fort Ocracoke, and is situated on the seaward of Beacon Island. It was entirely deserted. It is octagonal in shape, contains four shell rooms, about twenty-five feet square, and in the center a large boom-proof, one hundred feet square, with the magazine within it. Directly above the magazine, on each side, were four large tanks containing water. The fort had been constructed with great care, of sand in barrels covered with earth and turf. The inner framing of the bomb-proof was built of heavy pine timbers. There were platforms for twenty guns, which had been partially destroyed by fire. The gun carriages had been all burned. There were eighteen guns in the fort--namely, four eight-inch navy shell guns, and fourteen long thirty-two pounders. The steamer *Albemarle* left on Sunday afternoon, carring off two guns. I found one hundred and fifty barrels also, many of them filled with water. There being no water in the fort, they had brought it from Washington and Newberry (New Bern).

I landed the men at half-past one o'clock, and commenced breaking off the trunnions of the guns. While a portion of our men and the Naval Brigade were so employed, I sent Lieutenant Eastman in the launch to Portsmouth, where he found three eight-inch navy shell guns lying on the beach and one mounted on a carriage. They had all been spiked. There was no battery erected there, although we were informed that one would have been built but for our coming. There had been a camp at Portsmouth, called Camp Washington, but a portion of the troops were sent to Fort Hatteras when it was attacked, on August 28, and the remainder retired to the mainland. Portsmouth, which formerly contained four hundred and fifty inhabitants, was nearly deserted, but the people are expected to return. Those remaining seem to be Union men, and expressed satisfaction at our coming. Lieutenant Eastman assured them that they would not be molested by the Government and that they might return to their usual occupations.

There are no entrenchments nor guns at Ocracoke. The fishermen and pilots, who fled after our attack, have generally returned. I tried to destroy the guns by breaking the trunnions off with sledge and by dropping solid shot upon them from an elevation, but with little success. I then tried solid shot from a sixty-four-pounder at them, and in this manner disabled them. Lieutenant Eastman disabled the guns at Portsmouth by knocking off the cascables, and leaving them in the salt water on the beach.

After destroying the guns, I collected all the lumber, barrels and wheelbarrows, and placed them in and about the bomb-proof, set fire to the pile and entirely destroyed it. A lightship, which had been used as a storeship, and which was run upon the shore some distance from the fort, with the intention off subsequently towing her off and arming, I set fire to.

At half-past six o'clock this morning I started on our return. We met with no detention, and arrived safely with all hands at half-past 11 o'clock. I am happy to report that the conduct of our men and the Naval Brigade was excellent. Lieutenant Eastman and Lieutenant Tillotson and Lieutenant Roe of the Naval Brigade, rendered me most efficient assistance.

I am, respectfully, your obedient servant.

JAMES Y. MAXWELL
Lieutenant United States Navy

COMMANDER S.C. ROWAN.
UNITED STATES STEAMER PAWNEE.

THE WAR IN AMERICA.- FORT OCRACOKE, ON BEACON ISLAND, NORTH CAROLINA, DESTROYED BY FIRE ON THE 17TH ULT. BY THE FEDERALISTS

The capture of Fort Ocracoke was even carried in a London newspaper.

THE ILLUSTRATED LONDON NEWS Oct.19,1861
ILLUSTRATIONS OF THE WAR IN AMERICA
DESTRUCTION OF FORT OCRACOKE,
ON BEACON ISLAND, NORTH CAROLINA

On the 16th ult. an expedition left Fortress Monroe to take and destroy the fort on Beacon Island, near the entrance to the Sound. It was under the command of Lieutenant Eastman, of the *Pawnee*, and consisted of sixty-five men from Coast Guard and an attachment of sailors and marines from the *Pawnee*, in the ship's launch. The Coast Guard were on board the *Fanny*,which towed the launch down. The landing was safely effected. The fort was found deserted. The remainder of the day and the next day were occupied in destroying the pieces of ordnance found in the fort, of which twenty-two were rendered unserviceable. The torch was then applied to the boomproofs and magazines, and also the lighthouse on the island.

The conflagration raged furiously all night, the light being plainly visible thirty miles distant. After having completed the destruction of the fort, the expedition returned to Fort Monroe without the loss of a man.

After the fort was destroyed, schooners loaded with stone were sunk in Ocracoke Inlet, closing it completely to confederate commerce and raiders.

It is not sure at what time the residents of Portsmouth decided to evacuate the island. It may have been when David Ireland, a privateer and resident of Portsmouth, returned home reporting the appearance of Union ships at Hatteras. It may have been when they heard the big guns bombarding Hatteras, or when the confederate troops seized the hospital at Portsmouth or the appearance of the other troops in local waters. Whatever the case, Portsmouth was completely evacuated by the time the Union boats arrived at Ocracoke Inlet.

The Union forces not only destroyed the Fort on Beacon Island, but took charge of the marine hospital on Portsmouth Island and put it back in operation with Captain James M.Davis as doctor in charge. The hospital was used to treat the sick and wounded Union troops in the area.

Dr. Samuel Dudley's son Augustus being from the north, made special effort to be of service to the troops. (It is not known if Dr. Dudley helped at the hospital). There were still patients in the hospital in Feb. 1863 a time when there was no fire wood to be had on the island. Most of it had been used to build Shell Castle, the forts on Beacon Island and to build ships. What little that was left had already been used for firewood. Augustus Dudley agreed to let the hospital have a 45 feet long and 13 feet wide, heavy built and decked scow flat (then dry upon the shore) to use for fuel. Dr. Davis promised to pay Augustus $75.00 for the said flat, but in July of 1908 Augustus had never been paid. Augustus Dudley was a wealthy man at the beginning of the war with Twenty Five Thousand Dollars worth of property and upwards of Nine Thousand Dollars in cash. By the end of the war he was completly without property or money.

In January, 1863 Dr. Davis killed "a very fine cow beef" the property of Augustus Dudley for the use of the U.S. Soldiers Hospital at Portsmouth. The cow was valued at $20, for which Davis promised to pay. The next month Augustus furnished the hospital with 8 cords of oak wood for fuel, for which Davis promised to pay $4 Dollars per cord.

Augustus had remained loyal to his country and was subject to many threats and accusations and was once arrested, imprisoned and tried by the military authorities at a cost to him of several hundred dollars. (He was most likely thought to be a spy for the Union).

On August 17th, 1895 Augustus submitted a claim to the government for "compensation for his property used and destroyed by the union forces." He went on to say that at the fall of Hatteras into Union hands on 29th day of August 1861 the Confederate forces captured a good portion of his property (could have been the schooners used to flee Beacon Island) "for which there was nothing received, nothing promised and nothing expected." However Augustus felt that after the Union troops took charge he and his property would be protected since "he was in the Union lines every hour of the time from the fall of Hatteras on the 29th day of August 1861 until the war ended in 1865 and has been loyal to the U.S. Government every hour of his life."

The claim went on to say that in February 1863 Dr. James M. Davis, then in command at Portsmouth, bought from Dudley's store on Portsmouth seventeen new four damper stoves and three new six damper cook stoves for Federal camp purposes in New Bern, N.C. and Federal Convalescent Hospital at Portsmouth. Augustus agreed to sell the items at cost, the seventeen stoves at $20 each = $340, and the three at $30 each = $90.

Augustus also owned half of the stock in a store about 2 1/2 miles northeast of the forts in Hatteras worth three thousand dollars. When the forts were taken by federal troops the said store was entered and everything except one pair of shoes were taken by sd federal troops. February, March, April and May 1863 Dr. Davis employed the schooner ANNIE, 21 tons register property of sd Dudley, and a crew of two men in carrying and bringing sick soldiers, contrabands and supplies to and from New Bern to the U.S. Soldiers Hospital at Portsmouth. Davis agreed to pay $12 dollars per day for this service.

AUGUSTUS
DUDLEY,
SON OF
SAMUEL
DUDLEY.
b. 9 Mar 1831
Portsmouth
Island, NC,
d. 14 Dec 1912
Married
MATILDA
SWINDELL
on Portsmouth
between
1879-1880

On the 21st of February 1864 while Union forces at Washington, NC were being threatened by the Confederates, the schooner *ANNIE* was taken and used as a gun boat, with soldiers, artillery and ammunition on board. The said Augustus Dudley was put in command of her. He had a crew of two men whom he paid. On board at the time the vessel was taken was 566 bushels of corn which was taken and put in the commissary store.

In the summer of 1863 another schooner the *C.A. JOHNSON*, the property of the sd Augustus was destroyed by federal troops while it lay at a Shipyard in Washington, NC. The troops cut out the masts to use for flag poles at the officers quarters in Washington. One of the masts was dropped through the deck of the vessel, knocking a large hole in it. The troops tore away most of the side of the vessel trying to remove the mast, causing the ship to sink to the bottom. U.S. Marines in charge of a prize schooner that was without anchors took from the said schooner her two anchors and chains. One anchor weighed twelve hundred lbs., the other eight hundred lbs. each with chains sixty fathoms long.

The claim continued with a claim that the sd Dudley was contracted to furnish the U.S. Marine Hospital at Portsmouth with provisions for the year of 1861, and that he furnished Harbor Island Light Boat with an anchor and chain valued at Two hundred and fifty dollars.

Augustus Dudley put in another claim for the same damages on July 6, 1908, declaring he had never been paid a cent for any of the above damages.

If the damages caused to Augustus Dudley, a loyalist, were so enormous, we can only imagine the loss to those residents of Portsmouth that were for the south. Did those that fled when the Union troops arrived, have anything to come home to?

We may never know. Perhaps somewhere, someday someone will find in the attic of an old farm house, or fisherman's house documents that will give some clues, as did Mr. Bill Dudley of Climax, NC. Mr.Dudley, the present owner of an old farm house in Swan Quarter, NC owned by his ancestor Augustus Dudley found in an old safe within the house, the document presented by Augustus to the U.S.Government for the above claims. It is believed that he in fact never received any payment for his loss during the war of the Rebellion.

It was this war, the Civil War, that brought the greatest decline in the population of Portsmouth. Many did not return after the war. Perhaps they had nothing to return to, or perhaps they were tired, tired of storms destroying their homes, tired of being invaded by troops. Tired of war.

The days of shipping were gone and very little employment was to be had. People returned, only to leave some years later to seek employment. There were those who knew no other life or wanted no other life. They returned. They were willing to take their chances, believing that peace and harmony would once again come to their town. Return it did, and year by year the population declined so that peace and harmony became isolation and loneliness.

The Gilgos and the Dalys were among those that stayed. They were there to record the last few years. The interview with Mrs. Mattie Gilgo tells it all, the happy times and the sad times, then she too had to leave. Her daughter took a job with the Post Office at Cedar Island across the sound. Mrs. Mattie being a widow, moved with her daughter taking her youngest son Donald.

In 1860 the total population of Portsmouth was 568, with 100 students enrolled in school. There were 105 dwelling and 13 slave houses. 78 persons were illiterate. There was a Methodist Church and two grocery stores.

In 1870 the total population was 337 and only 60 dwellings which included 4 unoccupied. In 1880 the population of 222, and by 1910 there were only 178, with 42 households. Occupation of these householders were; 4 US LSS, 3 sea captains, 1 mate, 22 fishermen, 1 clubhouse cook and two merchants.

In 1950 there were 18 residents and by 1960 there were only 3. In 1971 the last two residents moved to the mainland. The Cape Lookout National Park Service now owns the entire Island and in 1993 the only former resident still holding a life-time right to a home on the island, passed away.

Shell Castle today is but a mound of shells about 100 feet long and 40 feet wide at the widest part. In the water's edge where Wallace's Channel passes, can be seen hundreds of Ballast Stones, bricks, parts of pottery and two beams from the warehouse.

Beacon Island is now the nesting ground for thousands of brown pelicans that migrate here every year. The island is made of sand and marsh grass, with no other vegetation. The water's edge of this island also produces small fragments of the past.

When I visit either of the two islands it is always hard to resist taking home at least one small piece of broken pottery or dish, just a little reminder of it's past, it's rich history.

CHAPTER 7

LIFE SAVING SERVICE

The United States Lifesaving Service was first established around the Great Lakes in 1847. It was not until 1874 that it expanded to North Carolina's Outer Banks with the construction of seven stations. Within 10 years the number of stations grew to 29.

It was not until December of 1894 that the station at Portsmouth was completed. The Keeper of stations was appointed and it was up to him to select a crew from among the local fishermen and mariners, because they were more familiar with the sea and weather in the area.

The first keeper of Portsmouth Station was one F.G. TERRELL. It was his misfortune, that at daybreak on the morning after his arrival, he went up into the lookout tower to check things out, for at first sight he spotted the schooner *Richard S. Spofford* grounded on Ocracoke Beach several miles from the station, with a distress signal flying. Now this put Chief Terrell in quite a dilemma since he had no crew or equipment to attempt a rescue.

There was not yet a station in the village near the south end of Ocracoke, only at the north end some 14 miles away at Hatteras Inlet.

Terrell decided this would be a good time to learn the character of the local residents, and help him decide which men to choose for the crew of the station. He asked around the community, and soon had five men volunteer. But this did not solve his problem, for the only boat to be had was an old leaky surf boat. The boat leaked badly, and they had to bail her out often. They would not have made it to Ocracoke if not for the

Postmaster of Portsmouth, who towed them the rest of the way.

Samuel Dudley Bragg, a pilot at Ocracoke met them upon their arrival in Cockel Creek informing them that five of the crew had tried to make it ashore in a yawl which had capsized almost drowning them all. All five men managed to swim ashore while the three remaining on the vessel decided to wait for help.

After learning from Bragg that no one had sent to Ocracoke Station* for help, Terrell decided to leave Jacob Swindell in charge of the surfboat, while he and the other volunteers left in a sail skiff for Ocracoke Station since they were still in need of equipment and more men. Once they could see the *Spofford* however, he decided that there was not time, for if they were to rescue the three men on board, they must do it right away.

---

*The only station on Ocracoke at that time was located at Hatteras Inlet, 14 miles from the village of Ocracoke.

He and Dennis Mason started out on foot to the ship and sent the other three on to the station for help. By the time they reached the vessel, it was almost dark. Terrell decided to try to reach the vessel by boat and hurried to the village to get volunteers. The Ocracokers were not very cooperative, for he could find only one volunteer among them. He asked for horses in order to return to the vessel right away, but had no luck there either, for he was told that they were all grazing.

This was not the normal reaction for such a situation from the natives, for they had risked their lives in many rescues. It could be that they were envious because Portsmouth got the new station, while the Ocracokers were still waiting for one in the village. However Daniel S. Tolson did volunteer to help Terrell, and got two men to go with him in the surf boat. Still, nothing he could say could convince anyone else to give a helping hand. Not knowing what else to do, Terrell again set out on foot to meet Keeper Howard and the Ocracoke Crew.

Meanwhile the sand was so deep that the mules had given out and the crew had the almost impossible chore of pulling the apparatus through the soft sand themselves. It was 8 p.m. before they reached the stranded vessel so rescue was not possible until daybreak. One man died during the night. The other two were brought ashore safely.

James Howard, Keeper of Ocracoke Station gave the following report about the wreck of the *R.S. Spofford*

"Dec. 27, 1894, reported to me by Capt. Terrel, Keeper Portsmouth station that there was three masted schooner on beach near Ocracoke Island. Keeper, crew tuck mules, apparatus, left station 3 pm. Fresh gale WSW with bad beach and distant about 14 miles which made it laborous. Arrived abrest schooner about 8 pm. The night was so dark and the surf very high, breaking all over schooner so it was impossable for men to rig up geer as they were snug in jib

for protection and only three men onboard. The others left
schooner about 12 N before that I was notified, in the yawl
boat, was capsized but all got to beach by the assistance of the
settlers of the island. So in my judgement it was best to wait
for day light which I did, making a large fire on the beach
abrest of vessel to encourage those that was on board the vessel. We all, with keeper of Portsmouth station staid on beach
all night abrest vessel..

About 6 am place apparatus, shot gun, six ounce line,
drop across Jib boom, before the man could get it, it blew of.
Got ready shot 4 ounce cartridge line drop abrest vessel
along side, the man got it. Readly hawled of whip rig, anchor
gear, sent of breeches buoy. Brought ashore two men, one had
died that night before. All was done that could be done. The
keeper of Portsmouth station was with me through all of the
proceedings. Left wreck 12:30 pm, arrived station 5 pm through
blizard snowstorm which made our jurny verry hard sum
of the men give out, rest chafe bad feet swolan. The next day
the men could not get their boots on. Could not send out on
patrol that night it is to hard for res to take care of 18 miles of
beach. There ought to be something don as we cannot stand
the long hardship. Our team (mules) is not fit for the service. If
had good horses in my judgement that we could got them saved
before night.

On Monday of the 30 the men better, keeper, crew with mules, surf boat left for wreck to get the dead body that perished on board Dec 27, arrived at schooner found that the cittisons of the island had got him ashore and tuck him up to the settlement and gave him desent burrel.. James Howard, Keeper

This was to be the first of many rescues conducted by the Keeper and Crew of Portsmouth station.

By the time the Lifesaving Service was established at Portsmouth, commercial fishing was the only source of employment. Those lucky enough to be considered for the service, gladly accepted. Names of men employed by the service are

Dennis Mason	Herbert S. Pigott	David S. Willis
Wash Roberts	Homer Harris	Daniel Yeomans
George Gilgo	Earnest Guthrie	William Fulcher
David Salter	James T. Salter	Joseph Dixon
Will Willis	Leonard Nelson	Matthew Guthrie
Melville Pigott	Joseph Fulcher	H.D.Goodwin
Alfred Chadwick	L.D.Williams	Mitch Hamilton
Monroe Gilgo	Simon Garrish	Gary Bragg
Benj.G.O'Neal		

Charles S. McWilliams of Ocracoke replaced Keeper Terrell in 1903. The station closed in 1938.

Life-saving Station Portsmouth, completed in Dec. 1894.

Horse stables of Life Saving Station.
Photo credit: Ellen Cloud

CHAPTER 8

LAND PATENTS

The earliest land records I was able to find concerning Portsmouth Island, were the Land Patents from the King of England, KING GEORGE the second, to one THOMAS NELSON dated 29th June 1738.

Pat.# 156; To THOMAS NELSON of Carteret County. 640 acres recorded Book No. 8 Page No. 17. reads as follows;

GEORGE the second, Know ye that we have given & granted to THOS NELSON, six hundred and fifty acres of land in Carteret County, beginning at the Sea Beach at The Great Three Hats Creek, then N32 E. along the Sound towards the Inlet 170 pols then N 38 E 290 poles, then S 35 ET across thebanks to the Sea Beach, then S W along the Beach to the first Station. To hold 29th June 1738

Pat.# 163; To THOMAS NELSON of Carteret County, 100 acres, recorded Book No. 8, Page No. 83. On the Core Banks & the Southward of Ocracoke Inlet.

GEORGE the second, know ye that we give & grant to THOMAS NELSON one hundred acres of land lying in Carteret County on Core Banks to the Southward of Ocracoke Inlet, beginning at the West side of the WHALEBONE HILLS S 23 E 175 poles, N 23 W to PAMLICO SOUND, thence along the sound to the first station. Dated 29 June 1738.

OTHER PATENTS ON PORTSMOUTH GRANTED
THOMAS NELSON WERE;

Pat. # 136 640 acres, Issued 14 April 1749, BK. 5 pg 413

640 acres on Core Banks near Ocracoke Inlet, beginning at a
stake in the side of a small creek, running S 35 E 125 chains to
the sound, then S 35 W 125 chains 20 links on the sea banks,
then to first station.

Pat. # 139, Issued 22 Nov. 1739, 640 acres, Bk.5 pg. 414

640 acres of land in Carteret County, on Core Banks, being
the Sand Banks between the lines of Richard Lovett and
himself to the Southward of Ocracoke Inlet, beginning on
Pamlico Sound about 360 poles from the Great Three Hat
Creek,Thomas Nelson boundry, then towards the Inlet N 38 E
280 poles, then across the banks S 35 E to Sea Side, then along
the sea beach Southerly to Nelson's bounds, then across the
banks N 35 W to first station.

When THOMAS NELSON died in 1773 the land was divided
among the heirs, all of whom were living at Portsmouth at the
time. Three pilots at Ocracoke Inlet, ADAM GASKINS, JOHN
BRAGG and WILLIAM BRAGG had married Thomas
Nelson's daughters.

CHAPTER 9

STORMS

Though the continual threat of storms at Ocracoke Inlet was great it did not slow down the growth of Portsmouth Island. The Islands of the outer banks were not evacuated at the approach of a hurricane as they are today. There was not enough time even if they considered it, for there was no warning. The first knowledge of an approaching storm was very rough seas, which would have made it impossible to leave had they wished to. Many times a storm-hit at night while everyone was sleeping without any warning at all. Since there was no time to secure property the loss was great both to vessels in the roads and to homes.

Though the hurricanes were not named and not officially recorded, records of the damage they caused can be found in unexpected places, some of which follow.

INSTRUMENTS OF PROTEST

October 30, 1749, a protest was made by WILLIAM DOWNS, Master, PHILIP GALAWAY, Carpenter, and GEORGE MAY, Mariner, of the schooner *DOLPHIN* sailing from Boston to Bath and then to London. The complaint stated that "storms, winds and seas" caused the ship to be driven on the shoals of Ocracoke Bar and finally, on shore on Ocracoke Island, and were responsible for all damages to the ship.

(Instruments of Protest, Deed Book 3, pg 24, Beaufort County Register of deeds)

"Violent storm about five years ago had carried away Beacon
Island, which was near two miles long, and all Banks here in
time may be lyable to the like,"
   (Letter to The Earls of London from Governor Dobbs. dated
   10th July 1757.)

John Wallace to John Gray Blount
Shell Castle, August 7th 1795

        I am happy to tell you the Good Nuse the Castle has
not suffered Twenty Shillings by the gale, althow it was the
worst and hardest that Ever was known at the Barr, all the
Vessels Cast away and most of them lost..
        There is a number of Vessels lost away from Cape
Hatteras to Cape Lookout..
        One thing I have to Say that is the Castle is worth forty
thousand Dollars more than before the Gale..
   (John G. Blount Papers, State Archives of History)

On Sunday night September 28, 1806 a revenue cutter
the"Governor Williams" that was to transport William Tatham's
baggage, instruments, and his papers of a whole summers work
to New Bern, riding anchor near Portsmouth was sunk by a
severe storm. Records show that a storm of hurricane force
rose with such fury that the vessel was sunk just two hundred
yards from shore off Taylor's landing. Lost with the ship was
all of Tatham's work and three men were drown.
Tatham had left for New Bern in a whale boat earlier that day.
He hurried back to Ocracoke Inlet after the storm, "such was
the scene of distress when I arrived, that we lay on our oars &
counted thirty one wrecked in one single view around us."
   (Survey of the Coast of North Carolina 1806-1808
   William Tatham.)

A severe hurricane struck Portsmouth on August 10, 1835. The storm was of short duration but did not pass over before doing considerable damage to shipping in the roads. Portsmouth was not well situated to give protection to vessels in such storms. Vessels usually anchored on the sound side of Portsmouth about due north of the present village. The wind coming out of the north northeast swept across the unbroken sound and buffeted the ships.

A far more severe gale struck on the 29th and 30th of August 1839. Old inhabitants stated that it was the worst gale since 1795. The sea tide completely covered the island during the height of the storm. **The water rose in some houses to an unbelievable height of twenty-seven feet.** All the gardens on the island were destroyed, the livestock washed away, and a U.S. Government boat house destroyed. Fortunately, there were only fifteen vessels in the roads, far fewer than usual. Four of these were totally lost, seven were cast ashore, two were saved by cutting away one mast each, while two fortunate or well handled ships rode out the gale. One master was lost with his ship in the storm. This is the only loss of life in the Portsmouth area.

(The History of Portsmouth, North Carolina - A Thesis - by Kenneth E. Burke, Jr.)

In October of 1837 a hurricane that came to be known as the **"Racer's Storm"** hit the outer banks, and proved to be the most disastrous storm in history.

A diary kept by a passenger on the Steam ship *Charleston* gives details of riding the storm out near Cape Lookout, how the passengers fought to keep the ship afloat and tied themselves to the ship to keep from being washed overboard after the windows and doors were torn from the vessel.

At the same time the steam-packet *Home* was wrecked on Ocracoke beach with 135 persons on board. 90 lives were lost and the beaches at Ocracoke and Portsmouth were lined with bodies. One survivor reported, "The scene the next morning was too horrid to describe. The shore was lined with bodies constantly coming up. All hands were engaged in collecting them together. The survivors in groups, were nearly naked, and famished and exhausted. The few inhabitants appeared friendly, but many of the trunks that came on shore were empty."

In the Carteret County Estate Records 1744 to 1957, State Archives of History, Raleigh, NC can be found the estate papers of one James M. Rolls 1841.

Rolls a native of New Jersey was one of the passengers on the Home that lost his life. Both his body and his trunk with all his belongings came ashore on Ocracoke Beach. William Howard, a resident of Ocracoke and acting wreck master buried the body, then applied in court to be appointed administrator of estate, then claimed the money and personal articles found on the body and in the trunk as payment for "washing, dressing and giving him a decent burial"

John Pike, justice of peace at Ocracoke petitioned the court to have Howard release the money and personal articles, exhibiting letters of appointment of administration to sd Pike from James Rolls of New Jersey, father of the deceased.

The following letters written by a regular vacationer at Portsmouth in 1846 tells of much damage there by a hurricane in September.

Letter # 1   Portsmouth Island, NC
                                                        Sept. 13, 1846
          Severe storm Monday night. Tide very high, raised instantly. Tide clapping against floor. The inhabitants say

that this was the hardest wind they had had in 20 years. The highest tide was at ebb. They say it would have been 1 1/2 feet higher if it had been flood.

Everything went ashore that was in the Rhodes but one vessel and a lighter. The captain, wife, baby and a girl nearly grown were on board. They succeeded in getting them from the wreck on Tuesday evening. They lost everything they had, not even a change of clothes. There is one vessel they do not know what has become of her. There were only two lives lost as far as I can find out. That was a vessel that went on the breakers. I saw one of the men and he told me she struck on the Outer reef and three men washed off. He was fortunate. I can count 10 or 12 vessels ashore and I have not heard how many at Ocracoke.

I have just seen Mrs. Dimock, she is very consequently, indeed. Mr. Tompkins is better. G. Bonner is down from Bath. He said it was very sickly there.

I have not seen anyone since the storm.

The bridge by Rumley's store is gone also one by Stirons' and the long bridge is gone. The ferry across is a boat from Rumley's store. Mrs. Moor's child has gotten worse.

A vessel just came over bar. She looks beautiful. The breakers run high today. At 12 O'Clock Mr. ? come over in his boat and took several people from their houses that have been torn to pieces. All the vessels that were cast away will remain as they are as they will not be able to get any of them off.

There is one from the West Indies, the money for her cargo is on board. All the men are wrecking every day but find very little. Some went from here today to save a boat.

There were 3 men drowned. The tide keeps very full. You cannot get a drop of water fit to drink. The rain water stinks so you cannot drink it and the well water is salt. I do not

know what to do for some water.
     Give my love to Mrs. Slade, Fanny and Joan Davis.
et citera, et citera

                                        Sarah Ann Clark

Letter # 2   Sept. 20, 1846
     The people are beginning to break ground. Mrs Moor's
family left today. They had a fair wind. Mrs. Diah Bonner
left Monday. Mrs. Joseph Bonner and Mrs. Potts will leave
2nd of October. Mrs. Grits' family will go tomorrow and then
will be few left by end of month.
     They say the Hatteras Coast is lined with wrecks. It
washed and blew down a great many houses on Hatteras, several children were drowned. An infant washed from it's
mother's breast and drowned. The *Raleigh* beached on Amity
Shoal, just over here last Wednesday between 12 and 2 O'Clock
in the day. The crew say it was Wiley Blount, he was mate.
The captain was sick in his cabin, his wife also. With great
danger a Pilot boat went to their relief. It looks distressing to
see so many wrecks. I am sitting by window and can count 13
without getting out of my chair. A vessel come in yesterday
with only one mast and very small sail.
     We had quite a gale last Tuesday night. It was warm
and calm all day. It made everything creek and pop and several vessels had to put back next day, that went to sea Monday. The Melville was one with several passengers.
     Mr. Taylor had been sick and is still. They think him a
little better today, he sent for Dr. Woodard. He come drunk
and done nothing. They have Dudley and Mery, sent for Allen,
he wouldn't come so Dr. Shaw took it on himself to come,
they will not let him prescribe. et cetera, et cetera.
                                        Sarah Ann Clark

The storm of 1899 was said to have done the most damage on Portsmouth.

Details of the damage to shipping are told in the chapter on Life Saving Service.

The storms of 1933 and 1944 are discussed in the interview with Mrs. Mattie Gilgo in this book.

In November of 1962 the Carteret county News Times carried a letter written by Ben B. Salter of Portsmouth Island, which reads;

"This storm struck the coast of Carolina, Sunday, Nov. 25 and has continued bad with winds up to 70 mph according to the weather station at Cape Hatteras. Extra high tides, three or four feet above normal now the fifth day of December, 1962. The outer banks have taken the worse washing ever, sand dunes washed and blown away and new inlets cut out through the banks here and there.. I cannot describe the horrible, dreadful look of such devastation. It is terrible to witness and I do wish that everyone could have stood on the porch of our fishing and hunting lodge at Sheep Island located on Portsmouth Island about three miles south of Ocracoke Inlet and looked out on the Atlantic Ocean Tuesday morning, Nov. 27,1962. Oh! what a sight.."

CHAPTER 10

MAIL AT PORTSMOUTH

Receiving mail at Portsmouth was almost next to impossible in the early years. There was no mail route, or Post Office at Portsmouth or Ocracoke. The only way to send or receive mail was by a ship that was passing their way. The mail came by way of Washington, N.C. and was held there until some one picked it up. There are records of mail for Portsmouth and Ocracoke being held at the Post Office in New Bern also. A list of persons having mail to be picked up was published in the newspapers published in Washington and New Bern each week. Someone from either Island whom might be trading in the area would pick up the mail on their way home. The problem here was that it could be as long as a month before one had reason to travel in that direction.

During the years of Shell Castle, mail was received rather fast, for Wallace and Blount had regular correspondence which was transported by their ships entering and leaving port. Usually at the bottom of their letters they stated by whom they were sending the letter. No doubt mail for the other residents were also sent along with theirs. However, after Shell Castle was destroyed by a hurricane, it was almost impossible to receive mail. On March 18, 1839 *The Republican*, a newspaper at Washington, N.C. carried the following letter.

THE REPUBLICAN
March 18,1839

From correspondent at Portsmouth;

Dear Sir,

It is not a little remarkable, that after all the exertions made here, to send memorial after memorial, to the three representives in congress: from Edenton, Washington, and New Bern district, all so much interested in the commerce passing through this district, we can get no mail, when at every road and blacksmith shop, through the country, there is a Post Office.---Mr. Shepard, I am satisfied, and Mr. Stanly too, I have no doubt, took an interest in this matter, and I was led to believe from a law passed last session, we were to have a mail. From conversation I had with Mr. Shepard, on his way to New Bern, when in your place, he was under the openion we should have the Post rout established from Washington to Portsmouth and Ocracoke, once a week, to commence next July. We shall see--Let it be remembered that 2/3 if not 3/4 of the commerce of North Carolina passes out at Ocracoke Inlet---Not less than 1500 sail of vessels annually---Yet no Post Office.

The long awaited Post Office was established on September 3, 1840 and remained open for 119 years. It was discontinued on April 11, 1959.

POSTMASTERS	DATE OF APPOINTMENT
JOHN RUMLEY	September 3, 1840
SAMUEL CHADWICK	September 25, 1840
JAMESS M. WILLIAMS	April 24, 1841
ABNER N. DIXON	November 2, 1842
D.R. ROBERTS	July 20, 1848
ANSON GASKILL	September 21, 1849
ROBERT WHITEHURST	January 28, 1850
SAMUEL E. DAVIS	March 18, 1851
JOHN O. WALLACE	October 4, 1852
HALLIS STYRON	July 16, 1853
SYLVESTER DIXON	December 17, 1853
WILLIAM S. STYRON	October 4, 1856

CARL DIXON, Mail carrier

ADCOCK BROWN Collection
(1935)

MRS. ANNIE SALTER, Postmistress

WILSON F. PIVER	January 7, 1857
PAUL J. CORNELL	October 18, 1865
JEREMIAH ABBOTT	November 17, 1865
JOHN HILL	Feruary 27, 1868
OSCAR C. RUE	October 22, 1869
MRS. MARY L. ABBOTT	March 19, 1872
MRS. PATSY WILLIAMS	September 21, 1876
WILLIAM O. WILLIAMS	November 28, 1887
LENA G. ROBERTS	October 5, 1897
ELLEN A. DALY	August 28, 1899
ELLEN A. WILLIS	May 15, 1901
WILLIAM H. BABB	June 13, 1907
JOE ROBERTS	March 1, 1919
MRS. ANNIE SALTER	April 1, 1926
MISS DOROTHY M. SALTER	September 30, 1955

By July of 1876, the mail was being delivered by boat from Carteret County. One of the earlier mail boats was the *POST BOY* out of Washington, NC. On July 29th, 1876, the *Beaufort Eagle*, a newspaper published in Beaufort, NC published the following,

"Our Eastern mail is now being carried by water all the way to Portsmouth, and during the winter season _____ irregular_____. We would suggest that the route be changed and the mail be carried by horse to the head of North River, thence across to the Straits and Smyrna, where the boat could take it to Portsmouth and same route returning. This would pass through the thickly settled neighborhoods at which, Post Offices could be established.."

In December of 1881, Portsmouth was getting mail on Monday and Thursday only, as were Ocracoke, Atlantic, Roe, Smyrna and Straits. (*Carteret Co. Telephone*, Beaufort Weekly, Dec. 23,1881)

In 1904 a gasoline schooner the *Meteor*, owned by the Beaufort, Morehead City and Ocracoke Steamship Company and commanded by Capt A.B. Styron ran the mail from Beaufort to Ocracoke. The Lifesaving Crew of Portsmouth went to the vessels aid, once in November and twice in December of 1904. Capt. Styron unacquainted with the channels ran the vessel aground on the same shoal three times.*

In 1910 Thomas Hamilton and Joseph Mason of Atlantic made the run from Beaufort to Ocracoke on the *Viola*,* and in 1911 Thomas Hamilton made the run on the *Hero*,* in 1912 the *Viola* was on the run.

The mail at one time left Smyrna, in Carteret County, stopping at Atlantic, Lola, Roe, Portsmouth and Ocracoke. When the road was paved all the way to Atlantic, NC the boat trip was much shorter and mail was delivered every day.

Names of some of the mail boats were; *"M" City*,

*Williamson, Sonny, "Unsung Heroes of the Surf" 1992.

Mailboat *ALETA* waiting to take on mail at Portsmouth.
The Author, her father and brother on bow.

Henry Pigott poling skiff to meet mail boat.

Ocracoke, Bessie M. and next the *Aleta*. In 1936 Capt. Wilbur
Nelson of Atlantic got the mail contract to Ocracoke. He
started his route with the *Bessie M*. When his boat burned to
the water line he bought the *Aleta* from Mr. Dee Mason. Capt.
Elmo Fulcher (my father) ran as mate and relief captain for
Capt. Wilbur. In 1945 Capt. Elmo and George O'Neal, both of
Ocracoke got the contract for the mail route. Capt. Wilbur

sold the *Aleta* to them and she continued her run until 1952 when Ansley O'Neal started the run on the *Dolphin*.

The waters around Portsmouth were not deep enough for these vessels. A skiff came out to the channel to meet the mail boat and exchange sacks of mail and take off passengers. Two of the mail carriers that met the boat in a skiff were Carl Dixon and Henry Pigott.

After the road was paved at Ocracoke the ferry began to run on a regular schedule across Hatteras Inlet and the mail to Ocracoke was delivered by truck. Portsmouth's mail was also trucked in to Ocracoke and then delivered by a small boat from Ocracoke. Maltby Bragg was the first mail carrier to Portsmouth from Ocracoke. He ran the mail for several years before Lum Gaskill took over the run.

Lum made the trip three times a week in his small flat bottom wooden skiff "Old Bonnie" delivering everything from tanks of gas to cans of snuff. His little skiff made its way into Dr's Creek where Lum hand delivered the mail to the residents. There had been no Post Office or Post master operating on the Island since 1959. Residents on the Island when Lum made his run were; Ross Salter, Fred Cannon, Marion Babb, Elma Dixon,

Lum Gaskill on porch of Post Office

Henry Pigott and Mrs. Burk. There were also several people living on the lower end of the Island. By 1972 there were only three residents on the Island and the U.S. Postal Service decided they could not justify the expense of delivering the mail to this isolated Island. The entire population (three people) got together and signed a petition to keep Lum from being "let go". How would the residents get groceries and supplies? How would they get their mail? Regardless of their efforts to keep Lum, their only connection with the rest of the world, he made his last run on June 30,1972.

Henry Pigott and Lum Gaskill delivering
mail and supplies to residents of Portsmouth.

CHAPTER 11

THE BLACK FAMILY

As strange as it may seem, there was never more than one black family on Ocracoke, Hatteras, Hog Island, Cedar Island or Portsmouth Island. Each community had one black family that not only lived there, but were very much a part of the village and loved by everyone. There were never any segregating rules that applied in the communities, except what the blacks themselves imposed on themselves.

Very few people have known or visited Portsmouth, without knowing or hearing about Henry Pigott. He was as much a part of Portsmouth as any historical landmark could ever be.

My most treasured memories of Henry are the many days I watched as he slowly poled the old wooden skiff towards the *Aleta*, in which my father ran the mail from Ocracoke to Atlantic, NC. There was one round trip daily. First stop was Portsmouth, where Henry would meet us, bringing the mail and the residents grocery and supply list. The trip continued and after stopping at Lola and Rew on Cedar Island and Hog Island the *Aleta* reached its destination of Atlantic. Here the mail was picked up and the orders filled by the local merchants who marked the boxes for easy identification. The *Aleta* then started its voyage back up the sound towards Ocracoke and Portsmouth. As we came in view, we could see Henry in his skiff polling out to meet us. I never remember having to wait for him. He had it timed just right, so that when the mail boat arrived he would be right there to grab the side of it and hold while the supplies were loaded in his skiff. (The waters around Portsmouth had shallowed to the point that only a skiff could reach the shore.)

The following information came from census records, tomb stones, neighbors and Ms. Mattie's interview.

Up until 1870 the blacks were not named in the census unless they were in a house of their own and free, employed individuals. Therefore we have no record of the family on Portsmouth until 1870.

Rose Ireland-Pigott was a slave or servant in the home of Earls Ireland and his family who were very well-to-do by the Island standards. It is said that Rose took a husband named Isaac. Legend goes on to say that he was sold in slavery to someone in Swan Quarter. (I have been unable to find the bill-of-sale.) It is recalled that Rose could be heard screaming and crying all over the Island.

Rose was the midwife on Portsmouth Island at that time, and was called "Aunt Rose" by the residents. It was a common practice on the outer banks to call a midwife "Aunt." After the war Rose and her family stayed on with the Irelands and are listed as so in the 1870 census.

IRELAND, EARLS	70	M		MARINER
MATILDA	68	F		
LOVE	34	F		SCHOOL TEACHER
DELIA	32	F		
MATILDA	26	F		
JOSEPHINE	25	F		
ROSE	35	F	B	
HARRIET	18	F	B	
SARAH	10	F	B	
DORCUS	7	F	B	
LEAH	5	F	B	
JOSEPH	1	M	B	

Lizzie and Henry Pigott

By 1880 ROSE has moved out of the IRELAND house
and is living next door. **Two of her children are still with the
IRELANDS and listed as GRAND CHILDREN. DORCUS
age 16 and LEAH age 14.** EARLS is not listed in 1880. Since
he was listed as a mariner, he may have been at sea. He was
not yet deceased, for in 1895 he deeds the property to
SOPHONIA GILGO, describing it as the "land and house
known as the Big House Place," By now Earl's daughter
JOSEPHINE has married THOMAS TOLSON and is living
in the Ireland House.

1880 CENSUS

IRELAND, MATTIE	79	F	
LOVIE C.	39	F	DAUGHTER
DELIAH	30	F	DAUGHTER
MARTHA	31	F	DAUGHTER
DORCUS	16	F	GRAND DAUGHTER
LEAH	14	F	GRAND DAUGHTER
TOLSON, THOMAS	35	M	SON-IN-LAW
JOSEPHINE	28	F	DAUGHTER

LIVING NEXT DOOR ARE;

IRELAND, ROSE	35	F	
HENRY	5	M	SON
NETTIE	2	F	DAUGHTER

**BY 1900 THE IRELANDS ARE GONE. LEAH is back in
the house with ROSE and listed as her daughter. If LEAH
is in fact daughter of ROSE and grand daughter of IRE-
LAND, then ROSE had to be daughter of either EARLS
IRELAND or his wife MATILDA IRELAND.** This would
explain why she and her family remained on Portsmouth when
all the other blacks left after the civil war.

Sometime between 1880 and 1900 ROSE changed her name from IRELAND to PIGOTT. There is no record of her marrying. Also her son JOE changed his name from IRELAND to ABBOTT after 1900. Why?

By 1900 LEAH has five children, RACHEL, ISAAC, ELIZABETH, (LIZZIE),GEORGE and HENRY. The father of these children are not known. Death certificates of Lizzie and Henry list Leah as mother and no father is listed. Ms.Mattie tells there were also Harry, Mozell, Met, Matt and Dark of which we have no records.

ROSE and LEAH are both buried in the cemetery next to the Keeler Place. ROSE died in 1909. MS. MATTIE tells that Rose went outside to roast oysters; caught her clothes on fire and burned to death. She was born Dec. 1836. LEAH was born 1867 and died March 19, 1922.

Lizzie and Henry lived in the house we all call Henry Pigott's House. The house and fence always looked freshly painted and the grass neatly mowed. Lizzie was born Aug. 28,1889 and died Sept.12,1960. After Lizzie's death Henry lived alone until he became ill, at which time Junius Austin of Ocracoke, who was caretaker of the old CG station, and later ran a ferry service to and from Portsmouth Island from Ocracoke, brought Henry to his house on Ocracoke. Henry was b. May 10, 1896 d.Jan. 5,1971. Both Lizzie and Henry are buried in the Babb Cemetery on Portsmouth Island.

HENRY WILLIS, brother of LEAH
PIGOTT, uncle of HENRY and LIZZIE

NETTIE PIGOTT, sister of LEAH and
Aunt of HENRY & LIZZIE PIGOTT

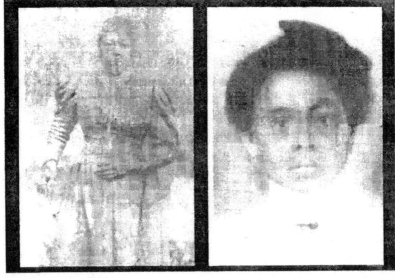

HARRIET (HATTIE)BRAGG
Aunt of HENRY & LIZZIE PIGOTT

OLIVIA MARTIN CARTER, daughter of
DORCAS PIGOTT & WM. R. MARTIN

CHAPTER 12

PORTSMOUTH SCHOOLS

Schools and education have always been an important factor for the residents of Portsmouth. As far back as 1806 there was already a school on the island. An 1806 map (see page 25) shows a large two-story building with chimneys on both sides, clearly the largest structure shown and is identified as the ACADEMY.

Another school house was located on "Straight Road", near the middle community. This school was located half-way between the village of Portsmouth and Sheep Island, centrally located to all school children living in the village, the middle settlement and Sheep Island at the south end of Portsmouth.

The last school to be used on Portsmouth is still standing and in excellent condition.

THE SCHOOL CENSUS
SEPTEMBER 1903
PORTSMOUTH, N.C.

NAME OF CHILDREN	AGE	MALE	FEMALE	PARENT OR GUARDIAN
NANCY F. AUSTIN	13		X	H. J. AUSTIN
LEVETTA G. AUSTIN	11		X	" "
LETHA AUSTIN	8		X	" "
CLAUDIA AUSTIN	6		X	" "
CHARLIE S. TOLSON	12	X		JOHN N. TOLSON
BESSIE TOLSON	17		X	" "
MILON H. AUSTIN	15	X		S. T. AUSTIN
MARIAH AUSTIN	13		X	" " "
LENTIS AUSTIN	10	X		" " "
LIZZIE B. AUSTIN	7		X	" " "
CARLETTE M. DIXON	7	X		B.R. DIXON
ELIZABETH D. DALY	19		X	CLAUDIA DALY

Name	Age			Parent
MARTHA DALY	17		X	CLAUDIA DALY
WILLIAM T. DALY	16	X		" "
CLAUDIA DALY	13		X	" "
EDWARD A. DIXON	15	X		GEORGE DIXON
HARRY N. DIXON	13	X		" "
NORA E. DIXON	10		X	" "
LILLIAN DIXON	7		X	" "
VERO GILGO	17	X		WILLIAM GILGO
RICHARD H. STYRON	15	X		JOHN A. STYRON
GEORGE S. STYRON	1	X		" "
ELLIS J. GASKINS	15	X		B. GASKINS
MENERVA GASKINS	12		X	" "
CAROLINE GASKINS	7		X	" "
BERTIE DIXON	11		X	JOE DIXON
GERY DIXON	8	X		" "
ALICE W. FULCHER	19		X	MANSON FULCHER
W. N. FULCHER	17	X		" "
JEROME FULCHER	15	X		" "
JAMES H. FULCHER	7	X		" "
EDWARD FULCHER	9	X		" "
CLAUGHTON FULCHER	11	X		" "
JOHN N. FULCHER	13	X		" "
MARY E. WILLIS	16		X	GEORGE R. WILLIS
CLATON WILLIS	13	X		" "
ROBERT M. GASKINS	15	X		GEORGE W. GASKINS
MIDORA GASKINS	6		X	" "
IRINE B. GOODWIN	9		X	CHARLES GOODWIN
JOSEPH M. GOODWIN	7	X		" "
ANNIE DIXON	17		X	E.G. DIXON
RICHARD DIXON	13	X		" "
DAVID ROBERTS	12	X		G.H. DIXON
—— RIBERTS	10	X		" "
ARTHER STOWE	12	X		GEORGE H. WILLIS
LENA STOWE	16		X	" "
KELLIE ROBINSON	12		X	JACK SALTER
MILTON ROBINSON	19	X		" "
MILON H. WILLIS	19	X		D.S. WILLIS
MAHALA WILLIS	16		X	" "
MOSES AUSTIN	17	X		S.T. AUSTIN
WILLIS	19	X		J.R. WILLIS

1. L.R. Charlie Salter, Ally Ricci, Floyd Gaskins, Elmo Gilgo, Russell Dixon, Earnest Salter 2. L.R. Elsie Slater, Leona Babb, Madelene Harris, Ethel Gilgo, Estel Dixon, Virgina Salter 3. L.R. Neva Salter, Maybell Bragg, Mabel Salter, Mary Snead (Dixon), Annie Mary Bragg, Alvin Harris, Tom Gilgo, Levin Fulcher, Henry Babb, Tom Gilgo, James Gilgo, Nora Roberts.

Portsmouth 1916 Children at Old School
Sarah Roberts Styron Collection 2/80

Old school on straight road near Middle Settlement *(Cape Lookout Seashore collection)*

Last school used on Portsmouth as it is today. *Photo by Ellen Cloud*

SUPERINTENDENT OF PUBLIC INSTRUCTION
CARTERET COUNTY, NORTH CAROLINA
PORTSMOUTH ISLAND
16TH MAY, 1894
VALUE OF PUBLIC SCHOOL PROPERTY
$25.00 INCLUDING LAND AND HOUSE

NAMES OF PARENTS OR GUARDIANS AND NUMBER OF CHILDREN

	MALES	FEMALES
R. ROBERTS	5	2
WILLIAM GILGO	1	3
WILLIAM ROBINSON	1	
AUGUSTUS MASON		1
ARCHIBOLD MASON	1	1
J. T. PARSONS		1
AMBROSE STYRON	1	1
ELIZA DIXON	2	1
CLAUDIA DALY	1	4
GEORGE DIXON	1	
SIMPSON RIBINSON	1	1
JAMES WILLIS	1	1
THOMAS TOLSON	1	1
VALENTINE BRAGG	1	1
EDWARD L. KEELER		1
SOLOMON DIXON	1	1
ELIZABETH GASKILL	2	
ASA MANN		1
EMELINE DIXON	1	
A.J. ENGLISH	2	2
JESSE NEWTON	1	3
DAVID SALTER	2	1
G.R. WILLIS		1
JAMES SALTER	2	
J. B. STYRON	4	
WILLIAM R. MASON	3	2
JACK SALTER	8	1
J.S. NEWTON	3	
	42	33

TOTAL STUDENTS MALE AND FEMALE

BIBLIOGRAPHY

Keith, Alice Barnwell
> John Gray Blount Papers Vol.I 1764-1790
> Division of Archives and History
> Raleigh

Keith, Alice Barnwell
> John Gray Blount Papers Vol. II 1790-1795
> Division of Archives and History
> Raleigh

Morgan, David T.
> John Gray Blount Papers Vol.III 1796-1802
> Division of Archives and History
> Raleigh

Masterson, William H.
> John Gray Blount Papers Vol.IV 1803-1833
> Division of Archives and History
> Raleigh

> N.C. Troops 1861-1865 Vol.
> Division of Archives and History
> Raleigh

Barrett, John G.
> The Civil War in North Carolina
> University of North Carolina
> Chapel Hill

Paine, Roger T.
> Place Names of the Outer Banks
> Thomas A. Williams, Publishers
> Washington, NC

> The Colonial Records of North Carolina (Second Series)
> Division of Archives and History
> Raleigh

Lemmon, Sarah McCulloh
    North Carolina and the War of 1812
    Division of Archives and History
    Raleigh

Barrett, John G
    North Carolina as a Civil War Battleground
    Division of Archives and History
    Raleigh

Simpson, Thelma P.
    1850 Federal Census of Carteret County NC
    Genealogical Publishing Co., Inc.
    Baltimore

Sanders, Rebecca W.
    1860 Federal Census of Carteret County NC
    Rebecca Sanders
    Smithfield

Sanders, Rebecca W.
    1870 Federal Census of Carteret County NC
    Rebecca Sanders
    Smithfield

Sanders, Rebecca W.
    1880 Federal Census of Carteret County NC
    Rebecca Sanders
    Smithfield

Sanders, Rebecca W.
    1900 Federal Census of Carteret County NC
    Rebecca Sanders
    Smithfield

Hofmann, Margaret M.
    Colony of North Carolina 1735-1764
    Abstracts of Land Patents Vol. I
    Hofmann
    Roanoke News Company
    Weldon

Mallison, Fred M.
        Fifteen Weeks

Gilgo, Julian
        Personal Interview with Mattie Gilgo
        Personal Tapes

Register of Deeds
        Records of Deeds
        Carteret County Court House
        Beaufort

Outer Banks History Center
        Official Shipwreck Reports
        Ocracoke and Portsmouth LSS
        US LSS and US CG Records

Carteret County Bicentennial Commission
        Carteret County
        During The American Revolution
        Era Press
        Greenville

        Map Collection
        Division of Archives and History
        Department of Cultural Resources
        Raleigh

PART 11
ORAL HISTORY INTERVIEW
WITH
MARTHA (MATTIE) DALY GILGO
FORMER RESIDENT OF PORTSMOUTH ISLAND, NC
BY JULIAN GILGO
JUNE 17, 1969
TRANSCRIBED BY
ELLEN FULCHER CLOUD
NOV. 1991

William Daly
Mrs. Claudia Williams Daly   b. June 2, 1844 in Dublin, Ireland.
b. Mar 19, 1857 - d. Sept. 7, 1914   d. Feb. 6, 1893 at Beaufort, N.C.

Parents of Mattie Daly Gilgo
Photo from HAZEL GILGO ARTHUR collection

Because of the foresight of Julian Gilgo, grandson of
Mrs. Mattie Daly Gilgo, a former resident of Portsmouth, we
have here a first hand account of the daily activities of
life on Portsmouth about the beginning of the century. On one
stormy day in 1963, Julian spent his day questioning his grandmother about Portsmouth and to our good fortune he taped
every word. After many hours of playing the tapes over and
over again, I feel that I have to the best of my ability, recorded
here the interview, word for word. The conversation starts off
slowly with a lot of coaching from Julian, but as the day goes
on, Ms. Mattie drifts into the past. Soon you find yourself
drifting with her as she recalls those treasured days spent on
Portsmouth Island.

THE INTERVIEW BEGINS:

JULIAN: What was your husband's name?
MATTIE: Monroe Gilgo.
JULIAN: What was your mother's name?
MATTIE: Claudia.
JULIAN: What was your daddy's daddy named?
MATTIE: William T. Daly, papa was named for him
JULIAN: How old was your daddy when he died?
MATTIE: 49
JULIAN: How old was your mother when she died?
MATTIE: Mama was 57.
JULIAN: You don't know how old "old man" William T. was?
MATTIE: No, I don't know anything bout that generation,
         only, I just know their names and who they were.
         That's all, I don't know anything bout um.
JULIAN: What was your sisters names?
MATTIE: Huh?
JULIAN: What was your sisters names?
MATTIE: Mary E., Ellen Agnes, Elizabeth D., Martha and
         William T. William was named for papa and
         Claudia was-----.
JULIAN: Who did they marry?
MATTIE: Ellen married Elzre Roberts (Sara's daddy). That's
         spelt E-l-z-r-e. He wasn't born on Portsmouth.
         Mary E. married George Willis from Hatteras.
         Daisy (that was Elizabeth) she married Oliver
         Gaskins from Hatteras. And I married Monroe
         Gilgo. Sisie,(Claudia) married Joe Babb. He was
         born on Portsmouth.
JULIAN: Is that all of them?
MATTIE: Yes, that's all. There was six of us.
         Sisie (Claudia), she was named for mama. She

was born in 1879. Ellen, that was the oldest one.
She married Elzre. Let's see how I got them
now-----. William T. Daly, that's papa
(grandpapa) and his wife was named Mary. And
his daughters were named Ellen, one of them.
Another was named Agnes and then come papa,
Mary Kate and George, they were Papa's family.

JULIAN: Let me write this down-----OK, your daddy's
name was what now?

MATTIE: William T. Daly.

JULIAN: OK, William T. Daly---where was he born? Do
you know?

MATTIE: No I don't son, I was only 4 years old when he
died- No I don't know. I know his people, don't
know when he was born

JULIAN: He had---What was his brothers named, do you
know them?

MATTIE: He was the only boy.

JULIAN: How about his sisters?

MATTIE: Well he had-----his wife was named Mary.

JULIAN: Mary?

MATTIE: Yeh.

JULIAN: What was her maiden name do you know?

MATTIE: No, I don't know, first there was Mary, then there
was Ellen, she was the oldest, I think.

JULIAN: Who is this now?

MATTIE: Ellen, that was his sister.

JULIAN: His sister?

MATTIE: Uh huh, papa's sister. Then there was Agnes, then
come papa, then George and the other one was
Mary Kate.

JULIAN: Mary Kate or just Mary?

MATTIE: Mary Kate, she was named for her mother, my
grandmother.

JULIAN: All right, that is your------.

MATTIE: Now that's papa's people.

JULIAN: Do you know any of your mother's brothers and sisters?

MATTIE: Yeh,-----mother's brothers and sisters? Yes that I do. My mother's name was Claudia Mc.

JULIAN: Claudia?

MATTIE: C-l-a-u-d-i-a Mc.

JULIAN: Now her sisters were------.

MATTIE: Let's see her mother------her father was William Williams, that was her father's name. And her mother's name was Esther. The oldest child was Elizabeth D.

JULIAN: Elizabeth D.?

MATTIE: Yes, Williams, and Aunt Pat's name was Martha.

JULIAN: What is this, your mother's------------?

MATTIE: My mother's sisters. Now that William Williams and Esther was her mother and father and Eliza Beth was Aunt Betty. We all call her Betty. Aunt Pat, her name was Martha. That's where I got my name.

JULIAN: These are your mother's sisters?

MATTIE: Yeh, these were my mother's sisters. Then there was---did you get Martha?

JULIAN: Yeh.

MATTIE: Then there was William T., he was the only boy.

JULIAN: Do you know your father's mother and father?

MATTIE: That's then, that right there, William Williams was mama's daddy's name and Esther was her mother.

JULIAN: I want your daddy's tho, I've got that.

MATTIE: That's it. This is papa himself and all of us. That's him, that William T. Daly. That's my

grandparents on papa's side. That's papa's mother
and daddy and his sisters. They are papa's
people, they were from Dublin, Ireland. That
William T. Daly was papa and Claudia Mc Daly
was his wife. Mary E. that was Esther and Ellen
Agnes, that was Tiney, and Elizabeth D., that was
Daisy and Martha,that's me--Mattie,and William T.
Jr. that's buddy and Claudia Mc was the baby.
That was my sisters and brother. There was only
one boy in grandmama and grandpapa's family
and only one in papa's.

JULIAN: Now, was that your grandfather that came here
from Dublin?

MATTIE: That's the one, William T. Daly.

JULIAN: And your father was William T. Daly.

MATTIE: Yeh, that's William Tunmnel.

JULIAN: Your mother was originally from Portsmouth?

MATTIE: Yep, she was a Portsmouthner.

JULIAN; Her parents were from------

MATTIE: She was just an American person.

JULIAN: Did William and Esther live at Portsmouth?

MATTIE: Oh no, they never come across, they never saw
any of that, they never saw any of papa's people.

JULIAN: I'm talking about your mother now, your parents.

MATTIE: Oh, my mother, of course. We lived everywhere
just about. Where ever he was transferred, mama
went. Ellen was born at Hatteras, that was the
first child. She was at the Cape, Cape Hatteras,
and Tiny was born in Washington City.

JULIAN: Who are these now?

MATTIE: These are my sisters, and Daisy and I were both
born to Fort Macon and buddy was born to

Hatteras. Papa was transferred back. From there
he was transferred to Kitty Hawk, where sissie
was born. There was not one of us ever born on
Portsmouth, not any of us.

JULIAN: Was he in the service then?

MATTIE: Papa? He was a telegraph operator.

JULIAN: Is that right?

MATTIE: Yeh---he was a Sgt. in the Signal Core. He was
the only man in the service at that time that could
take a message and send a message all at one
time. I've heard that from men who was with him.
Papa laid the first cable across Ocracoke Inlet.

JULIAN: When did you all first move back to Portsmouth?

MATTIE: Lordy--let's see---mama was born---mama and
papa was married in 1878, then he was ordered
up the Cape.

JULIAN: Do you know where your mother met your
father?

MATTIE: Right here on Portsmouth, he was a telegraph
operator at Portsmouth.

JULIAN: She was living there on Portsmouth at the time?

MATTIE: Yeh.

JULIAN: And her parents were living there?

MATTIE: Yeh, grandmama was living there. They were
originally from there, every one of them were.
Now grandmama's side was from Cedar Island.
And the place we stayed on Cedar Island was
papa's---their home, grandpapa and grandmama.

JULIAN: His name was William Williams?

MATTIE: Yes, William Williams.

JULIAN: Well, how did your father come across?

MATTIE: Papa come across to New York, and his father
found out. He was seventeen years old, he ran

away from the Catholic Convent and come across.

JULIAN: This was in Ireland?

MATTIE: In Dublin. Papa wrote his mama to let her know where he was. They learned where he was and they had the Ambassador over there and over here--The President sent papa back---to Dublin. He was only seventeen, and when he was nine teen years old, he ran away and come back.

JULIAN: Why did he leave?

MATTIE: I'll tell you why. I heard mama say, he had---they were wealthy people and they had maids and butler and hair dressers and all like that, for the girls. They were wealthy people, had a plenty. And that old Killarney Castle, I know you've heard it from me a plenty of times and read about it. Well that ...belonged to his grandmother.

JULIAN: What was the name of it?

MATTIE: The Killarney Castle, that belonged to his grandmother and she gave him his share. It was $15,000, I've heard them say. She gave him his share and he took his and run away and come back to this country. He got away from the Catho lic. And he had a sweetheart---Aunt Georgie's maid, he fell in love with Aunt Georgie's maid, that's the one next to Mary Kate, and of course----

JULIAN: Who is Mary Kate, now?

MATTIE: That was his sister, that was his baby sister---that was the one I showed you the picture---she was standing there in the door.

JULIAN: Yeh. Where did he land the second time?

MATTIE: He come back to New York. When he run away he was a stow-away aboard a ship--he come across---he went to school. He was educated over

there, with all the education you could get. He
was a priest---he didn't like the Catholic and they
educated him as a priest.

JULIAN: Didn't you tell me that they tried to make him
marry someone over there?

MATTIE: No, they wooden let em marry, they wooden let
him because that was the law. She was a maid,
her name was Julia. I heard um talk about her more
than once. Papa would sit down and tell mama
all bout her, how good looking she was. She
stayed right about the house. She was the maid,
Aunt Georgie's maid. Now he never talked much
about Mary Kate's maid. They had hair dressers
and butlers all about the house, the whole thing.
So after he run away, he went to school over
here. See papa couldn't speak good English. Papa
couldn't speak good English when he died.

JULIAN: Say you don't know his parent's names?

MATTIE: I knowed their names, but didn't know the
people. They were the Dalys, D-a-l-y, Daly.

JULIAN: Yeh, he was William T. Daly.

MATTIE: Yes, and buddy was named for papa, you see.

JULIAN: Do you know who your father's grandparents
were?

MATTIE: No, I don't know a thing bout um. I don't know
anything bout only papa's people. And honey,
papa went to school, I don't know how he come
bout to take up being a telegraph operator.

JULIAN: How come he come down from New York? Do
you know how he come to Portsmouth?

MATTIE: Yes, after he joined the service, he was sent
wherever they transferred em.

JULIAN: He just happened to be transferred to Portsmouth?

William Daly (1844-93) was stationed in the US Army Signal Corps office at Portsmouth in the 1880's. Many living Portsmouth descendants are related to him. He is buried in the Community Cemetery on the island.

MATTIE: He was transferred to Portsmouth son, it was
once a big town. If you want to find it, go to
Beaufort sometime and if ther's anyone in there
you know, ask em to show you the map of
Portsmouth NC. It's there.

JULIAN: Yeh, I've seen pictures of it----

MATTIE: Well son, it was a city one time. It was the
greatest seaport on the coast.

JULIAN: You'd never know it now though.

MATTIE: No honey, it was laid off in streets. That old man,
don't you know, they called em Sam Tolson--

JULIAN: I've heard the name, yah.

MATTIE: Well that old feller was the north key pol----He
patrolled the beach nights to the north key pole.
That was where he was born. There's the founda
tion right there. There's where the old feller was
born.

JULIAN: About how many people were living there when
you were young.

MATTIE: O-o-o-h dear Lord, there was hundreds. Ports
mouth has been a place in this world. I've seen
myself--- and I'm only 83 years old, and I've
stood on the porch an seen 30 to 40 vessels on
their way in. Just between Ocracoke and Ports
mouth, down there what they call Teach's hole.
Old Teach was killed there. That's where old
Teach was killed---was right there. The place
where he was killed, they call it Teach's hole.

JULIAN: Do you know any more in your generation that
you left out?

MATTIE: No-o-o, well Aunt Betty and mama had a sister,
but she died young---young girl. She's buried at
Atlantic somewhere. I've heard Aunt Betty---

where the beach is now is where Mr. Tom
Gaskill's home was, and now there was ---Mr.
Tom Gaskill and Dixon, and Stewart and Sol
Dixon and Mrs. Emeline Gilgo's mother, the
Rews. Now I remember their homes out there--it's
on the beach---now it's grassed over, now clear to
the telephone poles. There's bushes and grass way
out there--I've eat apples off the trees and I've eat
a many a collard from over there.

JULIAN: What about the big hill---how come---

MATTIE: Well, that was a vessel on the shore and that sand
coming there made that big hill. The sand blowed
on that vessel and banked it up, and kept on til it
made that high hill. Now it's not high like it used
to be.

JULIAN: What was the ship's name, do you know?

MATTIE: No, I don't remember, not for sure, what her
name was, but I've heard Uncle Billy talk about it
and mama and Aunt Betty. The ship come up
alongside the hill, you know, and the sand kept
blowing up. That's a tremendous big hill. And uh-
-her name was "Rebecca Flag", I've heard Uncle
Billy and them talk bout er, cause they remem
bered er. You go down there to Portsmouth, go on
the beach, sit right down on hill --- say this is the
hill--we set down there a many a time. On the
east side of the hill, that's facing the sea. They
wood be just as close---the ships, you know. The
sand wood blow um out, the wood works, out about
that high. The storms wood wash then out ya know,
the vessels. You go over there and take a look at
um. I've set and looked at um, a many a time.

JULIAN: How many shipwrecks are there that you can

remember?

MATTIE: O-o-oh Lor-r-r-d, how many? I don't know son, I
couldn't tell ya. I seen a many a one. I seen a
many----I saw in the inlet, there come three
vessels just about one time. One was loaded with
sugar, one with iron ore and the other had lime.
All one time, you could stand to our upstairs
window or on the porch and see them.

JULIAN: What caused them to go ashore? Get too close or
something?

MATTIE: They got too close, Portsmouth, when you're
coming along---when you come down by
Hatteras--Hatteras is due East of Portsmouth, well
when they come down and turn there at the bend
from Portsmouth to go on out to Beaufort, ---that
way or go to sea, you got to go by there. And
there's a cove---there was a cove. It's just a small
place, but they'd miss it. They'd think it's all one.
When they turned to go in that cove, that's when--
when it gets um. That's quicksand, that sand's
loose and they bury up.There's where the "John I
Snow" come in here, and we walked around er
with our shoes on. She was caring everything
from a automobile to a peanut. She had every
thing, jewels, furniture, clothing,--- everything
that---whisky---she had--that's the best scotch
herring I ever eat in my life. All kinda can goods.
I went on her 17 days. The days seemed long
some. The crowd of us went on her 17 days.
There was a landing on the beach. ____?____got the
automobile, and Capt. Charlie had some of the
furniture. Elzer had a chair--he had two chairs.
Different ones come aboard her at night, load up,

and carry it off.   That old black---uh--what was
his name--there to Davises shore?

JULIAN: Charlie Bowzer?

MATTIE: I don't know, I recken it was---it'll come to me to
reckly. His old lady's name was Elizabeth. He
come here and loaded his boat. He tuck it off on
his shoulders. Everything like paint and varnish,
stuff like that. She was a three decker.

JULIAN: How long was she, do you know?

MATTIE: I have forgotten son, how many feet she was.

JULIAN: Where was she from?

MATTIE: She was from north, and Dr---I mean Capt. Snow
was from---he lived in New York. He was the
owner of the vessel. The captain that was aboard
er wasn't the owner and as soon as she come on
the beach, why, Charlie Mc., why he sent a
message to Capt. Snow. When he come, talk
about a feast---anything that was eatable---he'd
cut the tops off the cans and say "folks help
yourself." He loaded us up, on top of us, cases
and boxes. He'd go there and sit them out- -say
"come on girls," cherries, tomatos, pears,peaches,
that was the 1st can vegetables I ever seen.. The
potatoes, they were in great big bags, like oats,
old big feed bags. He'd take his knife and split
it open and say "help Yourself." Them peanuts
were that long. Each peanut had three peanuts
inside the hull.

JULIAN: When was this, do you remember what year it was?

MATTIE: Yeh, it was 1906, Feb.---I don't know if it were, I
believe it were the 6th of Feb. she come ashore, I
believe it were the 6th. Monroe come home from
the Lookout the morning before, the 5th and she

come ashore that morning. It was foggy that
night. Alford would come after the mail. He run
the mail out to the mail boat. We heard em a
talking. Monroe said "there's a lot of talking
going on. Go up and see where it's coming from."
I got up and went to the window and I said, "He's
talking bout a boat come ashore." And he jumped
right up, jumped off the bed and slipped on his
pants, and he said, "come on, lets open the back
door and see." We could see her. When the fog
cleared off, you could see her sails. Oh, she was
in full rig, every sail that was on er. He said,
"Mattie there's a ship ashore." He went on
the porch, and he come back and said, "yes er,
she's right abrest the key post." He said "Jump up
quick as you can, you fix breakfast, I'll make the
beds, I'll make the beds----. "Sissie" said I,"brush
the floor." And Monroe said, "I'll build a fire." He
went in the kitchen and built a fire. I cooked
breakfast, by the time I got breakfast cooked,
Monroe had made the beds and Sissie brushed the
floor, and he said, "let's go," and we started out
bright and early. We went on the beach and for 17
days right on. I never missed a day.

JULIAN: Did it take them that long to unload it?

MATTIE: Yeh, everybody loaded, they come from far and
near.

JULIAN: Did it take them that long to unload the cargo?

MATTIE: Took them 17 days. Just as long as there were a
landing. She had worked down into the sand.
Then the sea would come and wash over er. There
was water in er you see, and they couldn't get the
stuff off er. It sanded up in no time.

JULIAN: Name some of the people that were living to
          Portsmouth when you left.
MATTIE: When I left?
JULIAN: Yeh.
MATTIE: Well honey, there were Jesse Babb's crowd and
          Washie's crowd.
JULIAN: Was that Wash Roberts?
MATTIE: Uh huh, and the station crowd and Harry and
          Margie, Annie and Theadore, Tom and Jody and
          Hub. Will Willis and John Willis. Annie Salter
          and all their family, Abner, Nora Dixon, oh there
          wers a lot of people. George Gilgo, Tom Gilgo----
JULIAN: Was Henry there then?
MATTIE: Yeh---when we left. You see Ethel, she took that
          examination for the post office. She was the one
          that made the highest points. She made 98.6, an she
          got it. Then she had to go to Cedar Island.
JULIAN: How come Henry come to Portsmouth?
MATTIE: Henry?
JULIAN: Yeh.
MATTIE: He was born there honey.
JULIAN: He was born there?
MATTIE: Yeh. Now I'll tell you how many of them negroes
          I knowed. They lived in the Dudley house. Old
          Dr. Dudley. There was Rose, Leah, Harry, Mozell,
          Met, Dark, Matt, Henry--Old Henry, Ike, Rachel,
          Ed, Lizzie and Henry, they all lived to Portsmouth
JULIAN: What was the name of the house?
MATTIE: Dudley, Dr. Dudley's, that's where they lived.
JULIAN: Was it a big house, where all of them lived together?
MATTIE: O-o-o-h yes, it was a big house. It had two parts.
          The chimney was in the center. Then they had a
          tomato farm. They taught school in the west wing.

JULIAN: Where did they come from?

MATTIE: The negroes? Honey, they originated right there. They were slaves.

JULIAN: They all moved away, except Lizzie and Henry?

MATTIE: They died. Now Mat and Dark and Ed---all of um, they moved away. Dark married to New Bern. Mat married--I'll tell you who Mat married, she married Dr. Barker in New Bern, and Dark married a feller up there by the name of Williams and then she had about 9 or 10 chillems. Harriett went to Providence Rhode Island, Harriett worked in a hotel. Aunt Rose---she built a fire out doors to roast her some oysters and her clothes caught afire and she burned up. Aunt Leah, she had high blood pressure and died.

JULIAN: When did Henry build that house?

MATTIE: That house? That house belonged to---that house, Harem Austin from Hatteras, that was his house. They come down there in the big time of Oystering. That big oyster catch down there, when they were making so much money oystering. My Lord have mercy.

JULIAN: And he built it?

MATTIE: Harem did, yes that was his house. Ed and Rachel bought it when he moved away and went back to Hatteras. Why, they bought the home and moved from the Dudley house over to there.

JULIAN: What were their last names? Henry's last name?

MATTIE: Pigott, they took the name Pigott. They took that name, old Aunt Rose and her husband. Her husband was named Isaac. They sold him over here to Swan Quarter in slavery.

Now I heard mama say--now mama remembered

that, her and Aunt Betty, they told, they sold
Uncle Isaac. Now there was screaming and
crying, twas a time. They sold em to Swan
Quarter. Old Frank Dixon and Ireland---Now
Ireland, that Ireland family, they owned Aunt
Rose. Aunt Rose and Joe and Leah, there was
Leah and Rose and Joe and Harriett, were slaves
and the others were born afterwards. They freed
the negroes.

JULIAN: How about the church, when was the church built?

MATTIE: Our last church?

JULIAN: Yeh.

MATTIE: 1916, that last church. 1916, that last one was built.
A storm come and blowed the other one down.

JULIAN: Did you say that you helped collect the money for
the organ or something?

MATTIE: I helped collect money for the church. I put the
organ there. The organ is mine. I gave $82 for the
organ.

JULIAN: What's gonna happen to it now? If the church is
ever moved?

MATTIE: The Bishop said it will never be moved. That a
church will always stand on Portsmouth. Cecil
Morris tried to buy it one time. I recken it's been
about ten years ago now. He tried to buy it and
he went down to Beaufort, was gonna intercede.
Some of the preachers were gonna sell it to Cecil
Morris---when they did, well we notified the Bishop.

JULIAN: Well who can sell it?

MATTIE: Nobody but the Bishop. There's nobody can sell
it but him. So Mr. King, he was the superinten
dent, and ah---we told him and he said, "Well
we'll see bout that."

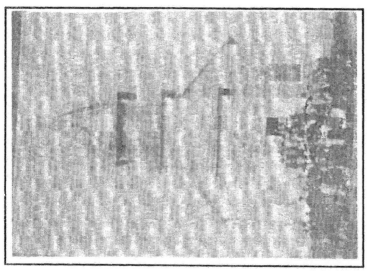

Present Methodist Church, built in 1916.

*Lionel Gilgo
Collection*

OLD METHODIST CHURCH, destroyed in 1913.
It was replaced by the present church.

JULIAN: Well can't the State sell it?

MATTIE: No, Capt. Charlie begged money and built this
church and it's on the conference land, where one
of the old churches stood. I heard mama say that
they had a great big church. The preacher was
named Hewett and they had a earthquake.*
Ellen was 2 months old when that earthquake was
there. I heard mama say they were sitting to the
supper table. That earthquake destroyed Ports
mouth. You talk about rocking a island. That was
the worst. Houses were destroyed. That done
worse than a storm. Storms were in the house but
twernt as bad as this. Twernt but two houses they
ever hurt. That was old man Jim Newton's, his sit
right down by the water, and the other one was
old man Charlie Willis and Missouri. That was
the only two I knowed, and there was never a life
lost. And I even seen one to start to the west end
of my porch and sweep right through my porch,
going in a great big circle.

JULIAN: The '33 storm went in a lot of houses there, didn't it?

MATTIE: Yes, but the '44 was worse than the '33. It was in
my house 22 inches and my house was 36 inches
off the ground.

JULIAN: The 1944?

MATTIE: Yes, that's when Cecil and Lionel and the whole
crowd was caught to Ocracoke. Cecil's boat was
right across the post office dock, laying right
across it, and Lionel went inland to work. Work
ing with Mr. Harmon. They was up in the woods.
Lord, it tore things up. It was in my house 22
inches and in the '33 storm it was 19 inches.

* See explanation of earthquake at end of this chapter.

JULIAN: How about grandaddy Monroe's side now?

MATTIE: Well old man Bill---old man Bill's crowd---now his name was William.

JULIAN: Who Monroe?

MATTIE: No, his daddy.

JULIAN: There was a lot of Williams wern't they?

MATTIE: They were all Williams. There was papa, grandpapa and Monroe's daddy, old man Tom was a William, little Tom was a William.

JULIAN: Ok, give me the names of your yunguns now.

MATTIE: All right, here's mine, Ethel Virginia, Cecil T. and Lionel D. and Donald Lee. Now that's the chillerns.

JULIAN: Where did Rita come in?

MATTIE: Rita come after Ethel, I wasn't counting her because she is dead. She was two years and two months old, she died in 1911. She was born in 1909. Her name was Margaret Rita. She died of whooping cough.

JULIAN: What was grandaddy's name?

MATTIE: His name was Monroe Willis Gilgo. He was born March 26, 1882. He was three years older than I was. We got married in 1905, July 27th. He died in---on Jan. 20,1927. He had TB. He was 45 if he had lived til March, he would have been 46.

JULIAN: Well what was his daddy's and mother's name?

MATTIE: His daddy's name was William and his mama's name was Emeline.

JULIAN: You don't know when they were born, do you?

MATTIE: No, Lord, I don't know, I don't know if any of that family knowed any thing bout old man Bill Gilgo.

JULIAN: Did Monroe have any brothers and sisters?

MATTIE: Yes honey, there was Warren and Tom and George and Monroe. There was four boys. There was five

MONROE GILGO

MARCH 26, 1882 - JANUARY 20, 1927
Husband of Mattie Gilgo
Photo from Hazel Gilgo Arthur Collection

girls, there was Susan Jane, Sarah, Lillian, Angie, Teressa and Vera. She had nine chillerns. He was 20 years older than Miss Emeline. She got married when she was 16. He come over on a vessel.

JULIAN: You know how old, old man Bill was when he died?

MATTIE: Yes, he was 79, soon been 80 when he died. He died May 2,1906, or was it 7--1907

JULIAN: Do you know what old man Bill's father's name was?

MATTIE: No--no--I don't know anything bout him. Now old man Bill was in the war. I don't know which one. He come there on a vessel, I heard Monroe say. Now he was in the war. But he deserted, he run away, I hear Monroe say.

JULIAN: That was old man Bill's daddy?

MATTIE: Yes it was his daddy. There was a crowd of those chillerns--there was---now I know of these--he had a brother--now he went to New York.

JULIAN: What was his brother's name?

MATTIE: First name was William, they called him William. They didn't know much about him. He never let none of them know much bout his business. He's got a big hotel in New York?

JULIAN: Is that old man Bill's brother?

MATTIE: That was his brother.

JULIAN: Was that the only one he had?

MATTIE: As for as I know, son. Bill never talked much about his family. Now he had a girl--one was named Betty, she married a Dixon in New Bern and there was another one of um married a ___?___. And Miss Julie, she never married, but she was killed by a negro on East Front Street. She lived in a house all to herself. And her papa lived in the front part of a big house and she lived

in the back---kinda on the back, and a negro
walked in the house and killed her---that was Miss
Julie. Now Heneretta--we use to buy milk from
her. She was a Gotdod. Now I remember that
many. Vera use to go see um. She would go up
there to see um.

JULIAN: What about William, in New York, know anything
about him?

MATTIE: He's dead. Monroe, he tried to find out. The boy
just took off and never bothered with them. In my
time, Monroe and I were going together then. He
come as far as Ocracoke and he sent for them. He
come in there on a big ship and laid off of what
we call nine ft. shoal. He saw somebody and he sent
for to go over there to see em. Tom, Vera, Susie
Jane and Miss Jen and I don't know---I think George,
all went over to his ship and stayed all day it was a
Sunday.

JULIAN: Was he by himself?

MATTIE: On the ship he was, the crew was ashore at
Ocracoke. He was on the ship by his self.

JULIAN: What nationality were Mr. Gilgo's people? What
country did they come from, do you know?

MATTIE: Not altogether, no---He was part Quaker.

JULIAN: Quaker is a religion, what country?

MATTIE: Old Mr. Bill couldn't talk plain.

JULIAN: What about William, on the ship?

MATTIE: He went back to New York and I don't think it
was too many years, we got word he was dead. No
body knowed anything bout em. Miss Jen, she sit
down and wrote this lawyer and tried to find out
something.

JULIAN: When was this? Do you know when he died?

MATTIE: No, I don,t remember
——I don't remember. I
know it was in the sum-
mer time.

JULIAN: Who was it come across
on the ship, was it Mr.
Bill?

MATTIE: Yes, it was Mr. Bill
Gilgo, come across. He
come from the West
Indies.

JULIAN: Monroe's daddy?

MATTIE: Yes, he come on a boat
from the West Indies.

JULIAN: And he was shipwrecked
on the beach?

Lena and George Gilgo
from Cape Lookout Park Collectio

MATTIE: No--no--She didn't. He left her when she was in
the harbor. When he met Miss Emeline. They
lived there between Portsmouth and Ocracoke.

JULIAN: Bill?

MATTIE: Old man Bill's daddy.

JULIAN: Where did he shipwreck at?

MATTIE: I don't know but he come to Portsmouth. I don't
know who he married but I know he had girls.

JULIAN: Bill's daddy weren't shipwrecked on Portsmouth?

MATTIE: Yes, old man Bill Gilgo's daddy, he was ship
wrecked. He wooden go back on the boat. No, he
never wood leave, he come ashore from a vessel
and he never left. His father and mother come
there and they stayed.

JULIAN: That was Bill's daddy?

MATTIE: Yeh.

JULIAN: They came from the West Indies?

MATTIE: They were trading in the West Indies. That
weren't where they come from.

JULIAN: Did old man Bill have any brothers and sisters?

MATTIE: Just that one and now I told you bout his sisters.

JULIAN: How about the house you had to Portsmouth, did
you all build it?

MATTIE: No, it fell down.

JULIAN: What one fell down?

MATTIE: Our house, mama's house. Someone must have
cut the post out from under it. They set it afire once.
Somebody did. Happened to see the smoke
coming through the roof. The carpet, the chair
and everything--just like the chairs were put
together to handle the casket, mama was tire
out_____?_?_____and that was the last I ever
had to do with the house.

JULIAN: Where was that located on Portsmouth?

MATTIE: Right down the road from where I stayed between
the store and home. It was there next to the store.

JULIAN: How about the one you and Monroe lived in?

MATTIE: My house was up the road.

JULIAN: You all build that, or did you have it built? Did
you buy it?

MATTIE: Yes he bought it from a fellow by the name of
Lawrence.

JULIAN: How much did you pay for it?

MATTIE: I don't know. He bought it, then he tore it up and
repaired it---fixed it up. Raised the roof. Monroe
did, before he died. I said, "It was your place to see
to everything bout this house before anything happened to you." He said, "I want you to have it painted, I want you to have all the weather boarding
taken off it and have new weather boarding put on."

Above: Cistern located on William and Claudia Daly's homesite at Portsmouth

Below: The remains of brick from foundation of Daly's house.

Photos by Ellen Cloud

He said, "I want you to fix it up so you'll have a
home, lookout now and keep the taxes up."

JULIAN: What about the boat he had?

MATTIE: That was destroyed in the 44 storm---thank God
for that. The boat cost---let's see---right about
$1,000 to have the engine and everything, out
into er. Then turned right around and let Homer
Harris have that boat for $300. Jody Styron
owned her. Jody got Himer to buy in. Monroe got
Jody to give him a receipt and Monroe turned it
over to Jody. Honey, that Monroe he cried, he
was just as sick as anything I seen in my life. I
said, "It's good enough for ya. I'm sorry you're
sick, but I begged you not to sell that boat."
Lorenzo Gaskill to Sea Level bought that boat.
Monroe was so sick, he went down there and got er.
Lorenzo charged him $500 for just the hull of er.

JULIAN: How big was it?

MATTIE: Oh, it was a large boat. He paid Lorenzo with
cash money. She never went in the water but one
time. He brought er home--he went down there
and towed er back home with the mail boat. And
the fellers helped him and they put it on the shore.
One day he said. "I think I'll go paint my boat." I
said, "Ok, if you want to." And he went down
there and got all inside of er painted. He worked
on it and got the inside painted, and he come
home about 10 Oclock and laid down on the
couch in the dining room. And I said, "Monroe,
what's the trouble." He said, "I don't know Mattie,
I feel the worse I ever felt in my life." I said, "Are
you sick?' He said, I don't know if it's sick or
what it is." He said, I feel the worst I ever felt in

my life." I said, "As soon as I cook dinner, you eat
you some dinner and go lay down." And he did,
went laid down on the bed and stayed there. Next
morning he got up and went back down there and
painted one side of the boat, then he come home
again, sd "Mattie, I laid down on the grass." I said
"Monroe, you ought not to have done that. If you
were sick, why didn't you come home." He went
down to the store one day, he felt a little better and
went down to the store. And Joe said, "Monroe,
lets go big mulleting." There was Eddie and Henry
---Henry and Joe Roberts, twas together and Eddie
and Monroe. Monroe had a brand new net, hadn't
never been in the water. Joe Roberts, he had one,
Eddie, he had one. They had 4 nets--and they were
them big row mullets. They went, and I said,
"Monroe don't go fishing." He said, "I ain't feeling
bad Mattie." I said, "Monroe you'll come home
soaking wet." He said, "No I won't get wet." He
had waders and he said, "I won't get overboard."
I said, "Well, what you putting them waders for?"
"Well" he said, "I don't want to get wet." So he put
on his waders, they come up to there, way up
under his arms, and he left. When he come home,
he come with the water squashing out the top.

JULIAN: Is that when he got sick? Really sick?

MATTIE: Well son, he never left the house no more. That
was his last trip and that was the only time his
boat was in the water, that day. They made $79
apiece.

JULIAN: How long was he sick?

MATTIE: He was sick 4 years, but he stayed in Norfolk one
year. He was in the hospital in Norfolk one year.

Above: Front gate to Mattie and Monroe Gilgo's homesite.
Below: Cistern located on Gilgo property

Photos by Ellen Cloud

And another year he stayed up there in the western part of the state.

JULIAN: It weren't TB all along was it?

MATTIE: Yes, he didn't have it bad but they kept him in that hospital---in the government---he was in the station. He never were turned out of the station. Monroe was just home from active duty. If he'd got better, he'd gone back to the station. He was sick here for a year and one year up state and a year in Norfolk. One year he wasn't real sick, just feeling bad, like that.

JULIAN: How long was he in bed before he------

MATTIE: Well he went to bed---let's see---he come home in December, he stayed in that month. He weighed 182 lb.when he went home from the hospital. I couldn't do nothing with him. He'd go out in the rain and I begged him to stay in. He'd go to the store and down to the station and around. The next December, Mr. Warren and Ms Sophie went down there and spent Christmas with us. That was the last meal he ate from that table. Now son, we didn't eat out of no dishes that he eat outa, nor we didn't drink outa no glass he drunk outa, nor we never used no bedding he used, and his clothes weren't washed with ourn.

JULIAN: How about telling me about the ship that come in the harbor there, with all that whiskey on it, that the Coast Guardmen went out and got so drunk on.

MATTIE: That---I recken the first one they cut up and carried on so was the "S Warren Hall," she came ashore in the inlet.

JULIAN: Is that the one the Coast Guard stood watch over?

MATTIE: No honey, that was the old "Message of Peace."

Blessed Lord, she was nothing but whiskey, beer
and wine. She come right on (chuckle) right on
up almost to the station dock. (chuckle) that she
did (chuckle). Henry and Joe Roberts had it
stacked up. He sold it. Henry, black Henry wers
on his right legs. (wasn't drunk). They made him a
millionaire (chuckle) I mind as well say. The
money they paid him---God only knows.

JULIAN: How come they got it off her?

MATTIE: He was smuggling it in. He was asked to go too
far with all that whiskey aboard. She was loaded--
deep--

JULIAN: How come it come in the harbor?

MATTIE: Why, Mc, Charlie Mc, he got word to em some
way or the other, to bring it---bring some in. He
and Wash, (chuckle)--when he got in there, the
Captain went up to John Wallace's, to have supper
on the other end of the Island. (chuckle, chuckle)
The men went aboard and took charge of
(chuckle) his whiskey.
(chuckle) Lord it was buried everywhere. It was
buried in the hills, on the beach, (chuckle) and I
recken there's some there today. Some of it
washed out by storms and tides, cause some of it
they couldn't find. They had buried it (chuckle)
but couldn't find where they buried it. Abner, he
had it buried in the wood house. He took the floor
up and buried it under (chuckle) the house. Then
the "John R. Snow"---Lord the whiskey was
aboard her. Beer and wine, there were barrels
stood bout that high, you talk about whiskey, --
was packed in straw.

JULIAN: I thought one time one come in the inlet there and

some of the Coast Guard boys----
MATTIE: That was the "Message of Peace."
JULIAN: Who was that got drunk on her?
MATTIE: I think they all did. I recken they all got drunk.
There was Wash--now I don't know bout Capt.
Leonard. I wouldn't say if Mr. Leonard got drunk
or not. There was Wash and Walter Yeomans,
you know he didn't (chuckle) touch any of it, he's
a Harkers Islander. Homer Harris, them boys from
up the beach, there was two of those.
JULIAN: Well, they had a good time anyway, didn't they?
MATTIE: Lord, have mercy, why he stayed around Portsmouth.
Walked around with his hands in his pockets.
JULIAN: What was his name?
MATTIE: Let's see now, what was his name----. The boat's
name was the "Message of Peace"--that was the
boats name---now I can't tell you and I heard it a
many a time. I think, by the look of em, he was
half negro, looked something like that, he was a
foreigner, he was, not our nationality. I don't
remember what become of the crew. It seems to
me like, the cutter come there and seized the boat
and him, they put him in jail and I never knew
what become of the crew. They may have been in
jail for all I knowd. He was in jail in New Bern
and the cutter come there and got the boat and
towed it away. She didn't have much of a load
though, when she went off. (chuckle) Between the
Ocracokers and Joe Robinson and Henry and that
station crowd. I'm trying to think, who was in the
station at that time---it was Sime, Leonard, Ed---
did you ever see Pennel Tillett? He use to be at
Fort Macon, he was from up the beach. He was a

great big ole fuss--scutty---he wasn't much taller
then me, but he was as big as he could walk.
Ruthford Sacrborough's sister's husband was there-
--now let me see, what was his name? Her name
was Elvira, she was a big stout woman and powerful, lord was she powerful, (chuckle) and he was
so slim. He wasn't much taller than you are---his
name come on the end of my tongue right then.
(chuckle, chuckle) He was kinda slim. Old Christmas, he took the gun and went up the road, he was
drunk and fell in the ditch. Somebody told Elvira,
that he was in the ditch. She said,"Yes, and I hope
he'll drown." She said, "I'll tend to em and the gun
too." She walked up that road and took em by the
collar and give it a twist, and marched em down
the road with em a staggering and she a pounding
em. Every step he'd take she'd draw off and lay it
to em. (chuckle,chuckle) I can just see em, as clear
as anything. (chuckle)

JULIAN: What about some of the things your youngans did?

MATTIE: That Lionel, that Lionel was a loud mouth. Cecil
wouldn't say much. Cecil was always quiet, just like
you and Donald. But he enjoyed what Lionel done,
what ever Lionel done he thought it was all right.
And he'd laughed, nearly die laughing at Lionel.

JULIAN: So, Lionel was a cat bird, was he?

MATTIE: (chuckle) Lord have mercy, I have seen the time
when I just as soon have Cecil and Lionel in the
house and nobody else, but just them two. I enjoyed
it just as well if it had been someone way off
had come back. My broom, I couldn't keep a
broom. He'd pick the straw out until it was bald
headed. Then, he'd get in the middle of the floor

and sing and pick the broom like a guitar. There's
a lot of fun in Lionel now. Not long ago, he
got on one of his go-horses and I laughed until the
breath was out of me.

JULIAN: What about the time he burnt the pants legs out of--

MATTIE: Oh, gee whiz, he was 3 years old, Monroe had just
landed from Norfolk. Of course, there was all his
clothes. Ethel had some of the prettiest under
clothes. She was all the time crocheting and she
crocheted the prettiest lace on her petticoats. They
were the prettiest. I missed em, I had cooked
supper and Theadore come in there and sit by the
stove. Monroe was on this side of the stove. They
were talking away, bout the hospital and how he'd
got along, and everything. I went to throw the dish
water out. I went out the door and headed for the
south side of the fence to throw it out and I saw
the smoke. And I said, "I wonder where that
smoke is coming from?" Well when I reached the
side of the porch to go into the kitchen, I saw the
blaze. Honey, he had lighted a big light wood
splinter and throwed in a box, I had in there
packed with material, homespun bed quilt lining,
stuff for my quilts---the top was piled on up.
Monroe had his pants hanging on the wash stand
close to the closet door. His pants were all wool
and they catched right up. they gave the blaze,
they were crisp, burnt that way. Well, he had to
wear them to Norfolk that way. What could he do?
He had orders, he had to go. Now his coat was all
right. I sent that to Beaufort, to have it cleaned,
but his uniform was bad. He had his watch in the
pocket. He took it out to look at it, the lid popped

THE GILGO CHILDREN
CECIL - LIONEL - ETHEL

Cecil and Lionel had married and had their own homes on Portsmouth
by the time Mrs. Mattie, Ethel, and Donald moved to the mainland.
                                    Photo from Leona Gilgo Collection

right up. It was a hunting case watch. He had
bought some towels, and they were great big
towels, there was one of them on the back of the
wash stand and that was burnt crisp. He picked it
up and said, "A brand new towel, burnt up." I said,
"You had better worry bout your uniform." The
bed quilts, the bed was afire. (chuckle) The carpet,
most of that was burned and that was a blistered
up mess on that wash stand. He never touched em,
never bothered em. I said, "Monroe, are ye gonna
let that scoundrel go?" He said, "Well, it's all over
now, it's already happened. It won't bring the stuff
back, not whipping em." I said, "If you don't, I
will." I went and got a silver maple, had a big tree.
One them white, silver maples. I come with my
switch and begin to cut it in em. He begged and
begged. Monroe said, "Mattie, don't hit em any
more, it's all over they ain't no need momicking
him em up now." I said, "All right, it's your loss
not mine." Ethel couldn't have a thing to play
with, for em. He'd take and throw um down the
chimney. She had a iron stove, that's home in my
room now, in a closet. She gave it to Sarah and
Bobby was about to tear it up. I said, "Oh, no you
don't. You'll not tear that up." I tuck it and carried
it into the room. Ethel has had it since her sister
died, in 1911 and I said, "I know where to put it,
you'll not tear that up." It had a little iron pot about
so high, and a frying pan and a little kettle and a
little stew pot. They were all on it, every piece of it
was on it. He took them cooking utensils and throwed
them down the upstairs chimney. Twernt no stove
up there and he learned that hole was there, and

everything he got his hands on he throwed down
that chimney, her dishes and everything.

JULIAN: Uncle Lionel would do all this?

MATTIE: Yes, Lionel would do it and Cecil would laugh.
They use to---you know where the school house is
now? That use to be where Jody Styron's mother
lived. That's where Jody Styron was born and
raised. It was a house built like mine. It was a big
house. She left some furniture in the house. Miss
Bessie got married and she went to---ah--she went
to Georgetown first--South Carolina, where her
Aunt was and Mr. Johnnie--. Then they went to
Augusta. He took them there on a dredge boat and
Mr. Johnnie was on board. ___?___was Bessie's
girl. She was about the age of Ethel, but she was
little. Miss Jennie went down to Wash's---she was
Wash Roberts oldest sister. So after she went down
there, they left a big table there in the kitchen and
chairs. Well, Mr. Cecil and Mr. Lionel, they'd go
over and sit on that table, chew tobacco and spit it
all over the place. One day Dave Salter come and
saw them there---so he goes in to see what they
were doing. He said they were sitting up there and
was spitting tobacco all around the table.

JULIAN: Sounds like they were good.

MATTIE: I've walked down the Haulover a many a time
looking for em.

JULIAN: Who, Uncle Lionel?

MATTIE: Yes, he'd take that shotgun and the boat and go off
and stay all night long. I told Emma, I said,
"Emma, is Lionel over there?" She'd say, "No,
Miss Mattie, he hain't never come."---she down
there working herself to death---. Well he come, he

come with 7 ole geese and his gun. He left his boat
to the High Hill and walked from the High Hill to
Emma's, with them 7 geese.

JULIAN: That must be where Lionel Jr. and Charles got their
hunting from. That's just where they got it from.
There ain't nothing they had rather do, than that.
Those ditches on Portsmouth---was there ever a
youngun that didn't play in them?

MATTIE: If there was ever any youngun that didn't, I don't
know.

JULIAN: There's been a many a soft crab caught in them
ditches, ain't they? On high tide they come up them
ditches. I caught a many one with a rake, myself.
I remember the summer we went there and stayed
in the house, mama and the bunch of us. I was right
little then, about 11 or 12 years old, I guess or
younger. I played right in the middle of them
ditches. For some reason that attracted younguns.

MATTIE: Do you know that's where Harry Dixon learned to
build boats?

JULIAN: Who?

MATTIE: Harry, that was Eddie's brother and Nora's. He
would take the barrel stays out of a flour barrel,
take um and bend um and fix um like he wanted
um. Then he'd put the bottom on to um. Then he'd
go round the island and bum a old clock from
someone. He'd take the works out of um and put
in the stern of that boat. That's where he learned to
build um. People would come from near and far to
watch em play and run up and down the ditch with
his boats.

JULIAN: What's the name of that creek between the church
and Henry's?

Above: Doctor's Creek, named so because Dr. Dudley's home was located here.
Below: Daly Cemetry, located near William and Claudia Daley's home site,
next to the Post Office.

photos by Ellen CLoud

MATTIE: Old Doctor's creek.

JULIAN: Was that the name of it?

MATTIE: Doctor's Creek, Dr. Dudley, old Dudley's creek. Dr.
Dudley was on that side. He built a double house,
with a big chimney between the two places and a
upstairs. That was the first school I went to, was Dr.
Dudley's house. The negroes lived in the East side. I
sit up over a dead girl in that West wing.

JULIAN: Well, who was that old man and woman that lived
down to the southard of you?---That had the warts
on her face?

MATTIE: That was Miss Liney, that was George Gilgo's,
Monroe's brother's wife. Now his wife was Jody
Styron's wife's sister and Tom Bragg's sister.

JULIAN: Is that right? I didn't know that. Why I remember her.

MATTIE: I recken you do.

JULIAN: That's been a long time ago, when I was small.
She's been dead how long now?

MATTIE: Yeh, she stayed over there to Cedar Island. Yes,
she's been dead about 26 years.

JULIAN: She hasn't been dead that long. I'm 29 and I
remember her.

MATTIE: I don't know just exactly when she died---I was just
judging from when we moved. It's been 30 years
since I left Portsmouth. We moved to Cedar Island
and stayed there 8 years. Then Ethel was transferred
to Atlantic Post Office, and we stayed there--
-I don't know, but it was close to 9 years.

JULIAN: Was there anybody else that lived between you and
her, when you left?

MATTIE: Between Liney and me?

JULIAN: Yes.

MATTIE: Milon lived there and Woodrow was over that way,

he sold his house to George Brooks and that crowd
from Beaufort. He bought Joe Griffins house and
moved it down the sound. Milon's, they burnt that
up when they burnt mine. And they burnt
Mr.____?____Gilgo's

JULIAN: Then there was a school house right across from
your's, then mama and daddy's.

MATTIE: Yes, then mama was farther down between Cecil's
and the store--the post office. That big house that
sit right there on the left hand side, that was
mama's. Then there was the cemetery right there.

JULIAN: Yeh. Well who's house was that right back of the
cemetery?

MATTIE: That was Tom Bragg's.

JULIAN: That yellow one?

MATTIE: Yeh.

JULIAN: What was his wife named?

MATTIE: He never got married. No, now Mr. Jody and Miss
Hud stayed there. She was Tom's sister. The one on
that side of the cemetery, the road goes right by the
fence, that was Ann and Theadore Salter's. That's
where Ernest lived and died.

JULIAN: How about the one right behind the post office? On
that side?

MATTIE: On that side? That was Theadore's. With the big
doormen windows on it, that was a great big house.
That was Theadore's. The yellow one, there where
you went and got that cup, that was Sarah's.

JULIAN: Yeh, that was the brown one, near Henry's. Back of
the post office, way back, wasn't there a old house
back there?

MATTIE: Yeh, that was where Sam Tolson lived.

JULIAN: Jody don't live back there somewhere?

Jody Styron and Jackie

MATTIE: Well, he stayed there til he died, then nobody remembered he stayed there.

JULIAN: It was who's in the beginning?

MATTIE: It was old man Sam's. Sam Tolson and his mother. His mother, now I remember her, her name was Mariah.

JULIAN: How about going down to the Haulover, who was down there?

MATTIE: That was Carl Dixon, and Mr. Byrum.

JULIAN: Who?

MATTIE: Mr. Byrum, from Raleigh. Down that way, right next to____?____right back of____?____. That was Byrum. It use to belong to Ms. Emeline Gilgo's mother, she died and left it, they sold it to Henry Babbs, he sold it to Gene Snow, I think. He sold it to Mr. Byrum.

JULIAN: Warren's was right on the Haulover, wasn't it?

MATTIE: Yes honey, the water is near bout up to there.

JULIAN: Henry's was back of Sarah's.

MATTIE: Now Henry's was right alongside of Dr. Creek and Daisy's was, use to be right in front of Martha's. Right in front of it was Daisy's house and right beside of Daisy's this way was Tiney's house.

JULIAN: Uncle Lionel lived in front of the church, didn't he?

MATTIE: Lionel lived on the church road, on the right hand side going towards the station. Now, Lionel had a nice place. Roy Robinson built it.

JULIAN: Who's house was that along side of Uncle Lionel's?

MATTIE: That was Joe Roberts. Right across the road from Joe Roberts was George Wiley and Mary Bet. That's where Claton lived. Claton Willis. Now the yellow house, that was Harry and Margie's.

Portsmouth 1909
top: Joe Gaskill, Mattie
Gaskill, Lillian Babb,
Claudia Daily Babb, Joe
Babb, Nora Dixon, and
Will Willis.
bottom: Henry Babb,
Beck Roberts, Elma
Dixon, Patsy Dixon,
(Elma's mother), Rita
Gilgo, Ethel Gilgo, and
Mattie Gilgo.
Marion Babb Collection

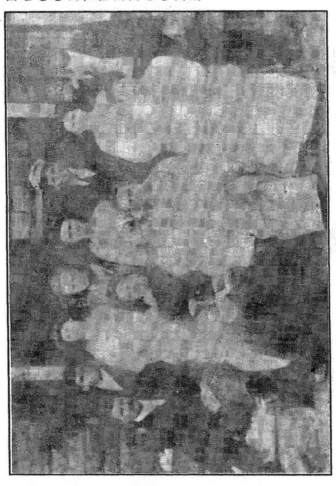

JULIAN: Right beside the church was Alma's? (Elma)

MATTIE: Yeh.

JULIAN: She was never married, was she?

MATTIE: No. no, Nora was never married.

JULIAN: Did Nora live with her?

MATTIE: Yeh, they all lived there together, Nora Eddie, and Alma. Lill married Jesse Babb. Nora never married, Edward never married and Alma never married. Neither one of the three of them. Beside them was Marion Gray and Lill and Edna Earl.

JULIAN: Who was that in the pretty yellow house on the other side?

MATTIE: That was Harry and Margie's. Harry was all the time fixing up.

JULIAN: I remember when I was little, that was the prettiest house on Portsmouth.

MATTIE: Harry had a pretty place, but it never was no pleasure to em. He never was allowed to go into the door with his shoes on his feet. He had to put on his bedroom shoes when he come to the door. He never took a bath in the house, they never washed no dishes in there. They never made nobread in there. They had a little house on the back and that's where he would go to take his bath, in that little house. That's where all the food was prepared to carry in the house to cook, then they ate and the dishes was carried out thar and washed. Honey, she was just as foolish bout that house.

JULIAN: Where was the hospital at?

MATTIE: The hospital, do you remember that old big cistern down there? It was to the southard of the station. Well, it's standing today. Son, I've played under that station a many a day. I walked right up under it. They had a brick walk that went----

Above: Lionel and Emma Gilgo's home on Portsmouth.
Below: Cecil and Leona Gilgo's home on Portsmouth

JULIAN: Were they any doctors there?

MATTIE: Oh yes, people were sick---I got a bedstead from out of that old hospital.

JULIAN: How many rooms were in it? Or was it set up in wards?

MATTIE: Oh honey, it twas laid off in rooms and wards, it was a big one. Lord have mercy, you could have dropped Donald's house down in one room. It was three stories high. It was a big one.

JULIAN: What happened to it?

MATTIE: The feller that kept the station, was overseer, set it afire.

JULIAN: Why, just to get rid of it?

MATTIE: Well, the kitchen was off there, and you come in the front door down here. The main part was the lobby where people set about. I've been down there when they had plays and entertainment. The kitchen was a gr-r-r-eat big one and it had a window, had a glass window, like that and you could raise it up and it had a blind on the outside to board it up like, and you opened that and raised the bucket up with water, out of the cistern. I've been down there with Aunt Pat and the rest of um, and mama and them and washed a many a day. Hung the lines full on the porch and yard, it was a big yard. Go down there in the evening and take them in. They'd be dry and hot.

JULIAN: Somebody said there were some tombs there back of the Coast guard Station, that goes back to the 1700's.

MATTIE: There's one right across the creek. That's one, that's where----that's the Dixon grave yard. And further over on the beach, there's Charlie Wallace, I know you've heard of him. George Wallace of

Morehead City, their father and grandfather are
buried there. And further out twards the telephone
poles is another cemetery. There's a tomb, I don't
know if it's out today, but it sure was out the last
time I was ever over there. Her name was Eliza
Wallace. There was another cemetery they call the
Ballast Stone Hill. That's where my land was, clear
to Ballast Stone Hill. That's out on the beach.
Then our cemetery, where they went to bury Aunt
Line, that was Uncle Billy's 1st. wife. She ask
them---there use to be a great cedar, that was a
great big cedar, the body was as big as a barrel,
and it was high and branched off----. There's where
she asked um to bury er. They dug all around it
and there was a coffin where ever they dug. They
couldn't bury her there. They had to bury her where
the cemetery is now. And he put four big cedars
around her. One on each corner. One of the caskets
they dug up, the woman was dressed in red. I
remember that, now I was small when Aunt Line
died, but I remember that all right. They dug that
woman up when they went to bury Aunt Line, and
this woman had a red dress on.

JULIAN: And you don't know anything about them?

MATTIE: No, nobody didn't. Now Ms Lizzie Wallace, that
lived in New Bern, where that cemetery we built,
were mama and papa are, Uncle Billy went to New
Bern and got the fence and fenced it in. Ms.
Lizzie Wallace had four chillerns buried in there.
One was named Lawrence, and Albert and the
other two I don't remember, one was a little girl.
There was four of um in there, and there was a
little white fence all way round um. The grave yard

From
Marion Gray-Babb
Collection

Elma and Nora Dixon mending net.

The Dixon-Babb family clamming.

is 100 sq. ft., it's square, 100 ft each way. There's a
Styron boy buried in there. I don't know nothing
bout em. Now Aunt Line, she was the first one put
in there, and papa was the second one. Then the
Wallace chillerns were buried in there, then old
man John Roberts was next and Eugene Dixon was
the next.

JULIAN: How about grandaddy Monroe, when did he go in
the Coast Guard?

MATTIE: When did he go into it? He went into it the 26 day
of March 1905.

JULIAN: How long did he stay in it?

MATTIE: He would have been there 16 years, when he died
in January, before it reached March. 16 years of it.

JULIAN: About how much was he getting paid?

MATTIE: He got $62.00 month. That was his base pay,
$62.00 a month. Now they wooden look at that.

JULIAN: What were some of his duties?

MATTIE: Patrolling the beach at night and standing watch in
the tower all day long. You never got out of that
tower. When you went up there when the sun rised
until it went down. Stayed up there in the cupola.

JULIAN: How often did he get home?

MATTIE: They wooden come home, only when his liberty
was. He got home every week, no---every ten days.

JULIAN: For how long?

MATTIE: He would spend the night, then go back next
morning. Monroe wudden allowed home when our
little girl died. No-o-, Charlie Mc wooden let
Monroe go home. You had to have a substitute to
go inside the gate and sign his name on a piece of
paper, before anyone of them could go to a funeral,
if any of their people died.

JULIAN: Did he get a substitute? Who was It?

MATTIE: Well sometime Uncle George substituted for Monroe, or maybe he gets different ones on the island. Just so a man went in there and signed that paper and stood them watches and went on that beach, why it was all right with Charlie Mc.

JULIAN: How many did they have at the station?

MATTIE: How many? There was eight, eight in a crew and the Capt. made nine of um. I don't remember what Monroe was at Lookout, but when he come to Portsmouth, he raised everyone of um. Course Wash was always #1 man.

JULIAN: What? Did he start out to Cape Lookout?

MATTIE: That's where he first went in the service---Cape Lookout.

JULIAN: How come he went there from Portsmouth?

MATTIE: They transferred em.

JULIAN: When he signed up?

MATTIE: Yeh, he stayed there to Cape Lookout 2 years, before he ever come to Portsmouth.

JULIAN: The station he was at, Cape Lookout, David Yeomans has now.

MATTIE: That Portsmouth station, you know, has been sold to some people to Raleigh. Junius Austin, he's from Ocracoke and he goes over there and looks out for it.

JULIAN: How often did they have to walk the beach and make punches?

MATTIE: Every night.

JULIAN: How many hours a night?

MATTIE: Soon as they went out at sundown and one of the men went North and the other went South. They come in at 12 Oclock. They had to cut the clock at

the station. They had keys to them key post to cut
the lock and you had better not cut it when Charlie
Mc was in there, one minute before hand or one
minute after. If you did he'd report ya.

JULIAN: They had to do this, even in the winter?

MATTIE: All the time, it wudden only summer time, all the
time---. In the day time they set in the tower.
There was a man went on at sun rise and stayed
until 12 Oclock, then another man took it from
12 Oclock til sundown. Now, I've been up there a
many a time, in that old tower.

JULIAN: They use to let you go up there?

MATTIE: Yeh.

JULIAN: You could go walk their patrol too?

MATTIE: Yeh, yes I went on patrols. Now, I didn't go too
many times south, cause---well maybe I managed
to go with um two or three times when he patrolled
the each south, cause that was a six-mile-go buddy.
Now I'd go walk the surf up and down til it was
time to go back to the station. We were allowed so
many minutes to walk across that beach to the
watch out and so much time to make that patrol.
Now I use to go north with em every night when
he'd go out sundown.

JULIAN: Did he ever sneak home?

MATTIE: Yes sir! Ah many ah night, he sneeked home. Him
and Mr. Hamilton.

JULIAN: What would they have done to him if they had
caught him?

MATTIE: If they had caught em? I don't know. They never
told on em. The boys all knowed that he went
home. They did the same---Wash would go home,
Homer Harris, he'd go home, all the rest went

home. All of um sneeked home off the beach.
Joe Fulcher sneeked home a many a time. And he
had a long ways to walk. When he'd get to that
grass, then he had to turn and go wa-a-ay down
there by the school house and then go up that main
road that went to the store, when he'd get by our
house, then he'd cut through and go by the cemetery,
where Dorothy lived, in a house on the other side
of the cemetery.
JULIAN: He lived back there?
MATTIE: Yeh. He'd sneek off. They would do anything, if
they could.
JULIAN: Is that where they lived---back of the-----
MATTIE: Yeh. They lived up there to Simmie Goodwins, Joe
Fulcher and Dorothy did. That was right long side of
Tom Bragg's house.
JULIAN: What? To the southard?
MATTIE: Yeh, bout to the South West. That's where Simmie
and Charles lived,--Then there was old man Ben
Dixon and old man Robinson and down that way
farther was Keeler.Charles Keeler. And Annie
Salter lived on the East side of Tom Bragg's house.
That was Kelly and Katie's mother. That's where
that path was made, from that cemetery, goes thru
there to Tom's ya know. We chillerns, going thru
there to Annies to play with Kate and Kelly. That
wasn't no road. We just made that, we chillerns.
We got the marsh all down til we killed it and made
that road, just going through there. That's where I
fell in the ice. There was a ditch just before you got
to Annie's garden. There was a ditch, it wasn't very
deep and had stones with a board laying down. I
went across it and it was froze, it was all ice, and

A Portsmouth Social Gathering
Cape Lookout Collection

down I went. L-o-o--o-rd, I knowed every nook and crook.

JULIAN: Did you all ever have parties or dances?

MATTIE: Yeh.

JULIAN: Dances?

MATTIE: Uh-hu.

JULIAN: Where did you have them? At the school house?

MATTIE: Yeh, they use to have um out to the school house. The parties, when it come to religious entertainment or something like that, they had that in the church. When it come to a festival or play or anything, they would get up, why that was in the school house.

JULIAN: Who did you say was the deserter of the war? What was his name?

JULIAN: Who?

JULIAN: The deserter of the war, was that old man Bill's brother?

MATTIE: Uh hu,---No, that was his father, that deserted the

war, that was old man Bill's daddy. He and another
feller ran away together. And they went out to look
for um. I guess they would have killed um if they
found them. They said that one of um, went up a
chimney and stood on the pot hangers---up the
chimney, you know they cooked in the fire place in
those days. This fellow, he searched the house, but
didn't happen to look up the chimney. That's the only
place he missed, they said. If they had caught em,
he wood have ketched the devil. Now who he
married, I don't know. I never heard any of um say.
That was in the time of the wars. The hospital was
open then. On Beacon Island, there was a big fort
on Beacon Island. Honey, we've been over to that
thing. That was a tremendous big place, by now it's
all under water.

JULIAN: Well, where did old man Bill join?

MATTIE: I don't know where he joined, I never heard
Monroe say.

JULIAN: Say he got fed up with that awful quick and left?
Did he come back to Portsmouth?

MATTIE: He stayed, he didn't leave. He fell in with somebody.
I don't know who she was. I recken Aunt Betty and all
them knowed, but they never told us. They'd only tell
us what they use to do. I don't know who he married
but I do remember that many of his sisters that I told
you bout was in New Bern. He moved to New Bern,
went up there after the war was over and everything.
He and the family of um. They went to New Bern.
What they went up there to do, I don't know. I don't
know anything bout that. There was Celia, Heneretta, Julie
and Hettie, that I know of. Hettie married a Dixon.
Heneretta married a Gautier. Miss Julie was killed.

JULIAN: Grandaddy Monroe's great grandfather is the one
that was shipwrecked?

MATTIE: Uh hu, I don't know anything bout em. He never
sit down and talked bout his people. I'd ask em
something and he'd say, Well I heard father say
such and such a thing. He'd never talk bout his
father's people. I don't know as he never knew
much bout um, cause Mr. Gilgo had but very little
to say---be around em all day long and never heard
him speak,---had nothing to say. Ms. Emeline died
in 1902. That was Monroe's mother, --May 2nd. He
went up to Oyster Creek and stayed with Warren---
when Warren lived up to Oyster Creek,there's where
he was taken sick. I was right up there.

JULIAN: Who Bill? Bill Gilgo?

MATTIE: Yes, when Warren lived up to Oyster Creek and
had that fish factory up there. And ah---I went up
there to see Mr. Gilgo, after Monroe and I were
married. They had three puppies, a old big dog and
three little puppies. They were hounds, and they
were black. That morning Mr. Gilgo got up and
went out on the porch and he claimed the dog
knocked his father, but that didn't happen. He had a
stroke. He never was his self no more. He had a
stroke. George went after em and brought him home.
Then George wasn't married. He never married Line
until after his father died. He stayed there in the
house by himself for a long time. He never married
Line until---Lord, I don't know how old Line was--
she was about 40 some odd, when she married
George Gilgo. Ms Line was old. She was married
in the Methodist Church as I remember. She was the
only one of em that was married in a church. I think

she was married on a Saturday night.

JULIAN: Did you say they can never touch the church to Portsmouth?

MATTIE: Yes, they had a Primitive Baptist----------

JULIAN: No, what I mean is---can they do away with it?

MATTIE: No, the Bishop wrote Rhoda and them, that they would never remove the Methodist Church from Portsmouth.

JULIAN: What I was thinking about, was the organ.

MATTIE: That organ is mine.

JULIAN: Do you have papers for it?

MATTIE: Yep.

JULIAN: Who's gonna get them when you're gone?

MATTIE: I don't know.

JULIAN: Well, if nobody else is more important than me, how about---can I have them?

MATTIE: I don't care. I thought I'd write the Bishop and ask him bout the church. If it were to be sold, where everybody had moved away, and they've taken it over for *wildlife, that ah---explain to em--tell em about the organ, that was mine, and ask him if I could remove it from the church.

JULIAN: Well you can remove it, can't you?

MATTIE: Yes, by his orders. I've got to notify the Bishop that I want to take it away from there.

JULIAN: Even tho you put it there?

MATTIE: It's on the conference land, that church is. It belongs to the conference.

JULIAN: What do you have, sorta like a bill of sale?

MATTIE: No, I just have a receipt for the organ and a certificate.

JULIAN: See, that's what I was thinking, you know every body has left now--------------------

MATTIE: Well now, they might sell it. You know there is so
        many people go there in the summer time---goes to
        Portsmouth in the summer time. The fellers that own
        them houses, they go down there in the summer
        time and stay all summer, til it's time for the
        chillerns to go back to school.

JULIAN: Well, I didn't want it to get gone, somebody to take
        it, you see. If anything happens, I want it.

MATTIE: The organ plays. It's got the prettiest tone to it.
        Prettiest tone. I had one come from the W.W.
        Kimber Co. Mine come from there. I had one.
        Monroe come home one day, said, "Mattie"--so ah-
        "Are you gonna keep that organ?" I said, "Why yes,
        I'm gonna keep it, it's mine. I bought it, I'm gonna
        keep it." I sewed for my organ and paid for it. He
        said, "Mattie, there's a man at the station, from
        Elizabeth City, brought some pianos to Ocracoke,
        thinking he could sell them. If you'll give me that
        organ and let me trade it in, I'll buy you a piano."
        I said, "I don't know so much bout that." He was to
        work, working on the living room, he said, "Well
        think it over, if you'll give me that organ, I'll buy
        you a piano." So, I thought to myself, I was in the
        kitchen, and I thought to myself, "I recken that's
        about the best thing I can do. I'll get that much outa
        it." And he come home and said, "Mattie, the man's
        to the station and wants to know if you'll trade." I
        paid $100 for my organ and he paid $500 and my
        organ for the piano. The piano come from the
        Adur??? piano co. He come home and he said,
        "Have you thought it over." I said, "Yes, I'll take
        the piano." He said, "Ok, but I'm not gonna take the
        organ out of the house till the piano is put in it.

ETHEL GILGO

When he brings the piano and delivers it to the
house, then we'll take the box that the piano come
in to box the organ, and he can take that right on to
Ocracoke with em." So I said, "OK" By Jumpey,
bout 1 Oclock, I recken it was, right bout 1 or 2
Oclock, he come in and said, "Mattie,where's that
hammer?" I said, "It's in your tool box, out in the
little house." So he went out and got the hammer
and took down a panel of the fence, so he could get
the cart through, from the station, the cart. He
backed it up to the porch. I looked out and said,
"That's my piano." Ethel jumped right up and
throwed her arms up and said, "It's mine." I said,
"Yeh, that's the way to do it." Monroe said,"If you
can learn to play it, the piano is yourn." And honey,
she learned to knock the keys outa the thing. She
wern't a long time learning either. That night after
they put it in the house. Janie Roberts and her
daughter and a crowd come over from the station.
They all come up to the house to see Janie play.
Janie played. She come up there and she said,
"Mattie, you've got a good piano." and I said,
"Do you think so?" And she said, "Yes, it's got a
good tone." said, "You've got a nice piano."

JULIAN: Tell me about the broach that you've got. That
necklace that's over 300 years old. Who give you
that?

MATTIE: Mama gave it to me. That was Sgt. Smith's great
grandmother's.

JULIAN: Who was Sgt. Smith?

MATTIE: He was one of the fellers that worked with papa.

JULIAN: In the service?

MATTIE: Un hu. His wife died---it was handed down from

generation to generation. She had the earrings and
the pin, she had the whole thing. When his wife
died---mama and papa married---Ms Smith, before
she died, she and Sgt. Smith gave it to mama as a
bridal present. Mama had that, she had a ring, she
had a pickle dish, that was just as pretty as it
could be. It was all kind of colors. What they called
them days, I don't know what they call it these days,
but they called it Jellica ware. I saw some over to
Williamsburg the other day, that reminded me of it.
She had a cake plate bout that big round, and it's got
a wreath all the way round it, of rose buds and green
leaves. It's just as pretty as it can be and as white as
snow.

JULIAN: Where is it now?

MATTIE: Ethel has it. Ethel has the pickle dish and the cake
plate.

JULIAN: How about the tea pot that Ethel's got, who's was that ?

MATTIE: They,---they are mine

JULIAN: That tea pot that Esther's got?

MATTIE: Yeh, that tea pot, that's down there to Esther's,
that white one with the gold ban, that's mine.

JULIAN: How old is that?

MATTIE: I don't know exactly. that was Hannah Robert's---
when she married David Styron, he lived up on the
other end of the Island,----they did. When they got
married, some of the back generations of David
Styron's gave her a set. They were 136 pieces of
that. When Beulah Gaskins, Holloway's sister,
married Little____?___, she broke and destroyed all
but a cake plate, a platter and that pot. The night
before he died, I sat up by him on a Monday night,
Hannah and myself. And he was laying there on the

bed and Hannah was sitting along side of the bad
and I was sitting side of em. He said,"Mattie." I
said, "yeh." I thought he was asleep. Hannah said,
"Well buddy, I thought you was asleep." "No," he
said, "I can't go to sleep, I look at my house and
see everything broke up and destroyed. I get so
mad, so damn mad," that's what he said, "I get so
damn mad, if I had ten years off my head, I'd put
the blocks in the air and the roof on the ground." ---
---And he would too.

JULIAN: When did they get married?

MATTIE: Who?

JULIAN: Hannah, the one that owned that tea pot.

MATTIE: Lord, I recken that tea pot--son--, is 50 years old.
I recken. Now Dave Styron was an old man. Patsy
Styron's don, old Aunt Patsy Styron. She lived on
the other end of the Island.

JULIAN: Well how about that cup that you give us there.
That was Rita's?

MATTIE: That came out of the "Avoin." That was a ship that
come on the beach. Now she was loaded with iron
ore. That was a great big ole long iron ship.

JULIAN: Who was the captain?

MATTIE: I forgot son.

JULIAN: Did he give it to Monroe?

MATTIE: No, the mate, the mate on er give---he give---there
was two little dishes---platters about that long,
there was whisky,---a bottle of whisky right on the
bottom of them dishes. And it said,"Watson, Watson
Whisky." He gave Rita one. He ask Monroe how
many chillerns he had. Monroe said, "I've got two
little girls." And he said, "Monroe. I want you to
take these two little dishes and give one to each of

your little girls. And these cups and these two
dishes." And Monroe brought um home and I tuck
um. That was Rita's, that cup.

JULIAN: What happened to the platters?

MATTIE: That Mr. Lionel broke one and I don't remember
who broke the other one. They were just as white
as snow, only that bottle of whisky was right in the
middle and that was black. What else was aboard
her, I don't know. The mate gave Mr. Charlie and
the crew the food, the grub that was aboard er.

JULIAN: When was this? What year was it, do you remember?

MATTIE: Let's see----it had to be about 1910, because Rita
died the next year, 1911. It had to be 1911, it had to
be. They saved the crew off er. They carried all that
apparatus from the station over to the beach in a
great long wagon. All that crew went on the wagon
and the beach apparatus, the breaches buoy and life
car. There was a woman and little child aboard er.
It was the Captain's wife and little baby. They saved
them, they saved them all. Ocracoke got the credit.
Everything that happened to Portsmouth, the
Portsmouth crowd was the ones that done all the
work and looked after the crew and saved them,
while Ocracoke slept.

END OF TAPE

Note; Reference Earthquake

When I first heard Ms. Mattie tell about the earthquake, I tried to think what took place that made them think there was an earthquake since I had never heard of such on the outer banks. Shortly afterwards while searching through lighthouse records I stumbled on the following information.

LIGHTHOUSE BOARD REPORT

EARTHQUAKE

Aug 31, 1886 The quake apparently was centered in the vicinity of Charleston, SC since that was the area hardest hit. The effects of the quake was felt all along the east coast and coast and a number of lighthouses were shaken.

CAPE HATTERAS

The keeper reports that he felt an earthquake shock on Aug 31, at 9:50 p.m. local time. The shock lasted from 10 to 15 seconds. It was accompanied by a rumbling noise. There were four shocks. They were severe enough to slightly crack the storm panes in the lantern tower. The 2nd shock occurred at 10 O:Clock, lasted about six seconds and was very light. The third shock occurred at 10:07, lasted about 10 seconds, and was moderate. The 4th shock occurred at 10:29, lasted about 6 seconds, and was very light. Its force was sufficient to set suspended objects swinging and to overthrow light objects. He further states that it sounded like a rumbling noise coming up the tower.The tower would tremble and sway backward and forward like a tree shaken by the wind. The shock was so strong that we could not keep our backs against the wall. It would throw us right from it. The swinging was from north-east to south- west.On September 3 another slight shock was felt at 11:05 p.m. which lasted about three seconds.

I hope this book has brought you a little closer to understanding how people could live on an Island infested with mosquitoes, without electricity and indoor plumbing. The solitude and tranquility more than make up for the lack of those modern conveniences.

I have had the pleasure on two different occasions to tape an interview with Cicel Gilgo, son of Ms. Mattie Gilgo. Our favorite night time entertainment while on Portsmouth Island, is to play these tapes for any guest that may be staying with us. His soft spoken words and occasional chuckle as he relates stories and events on Portsmouth Island keeps everyone mesmerized and brings this deserted island back to life.

Perhaps one day I will share some of his stories in another book for everyone to enjoy.

Ellen F. Cloud